TO FIND HOPE

MOTHER TERESA

EXPERIENCING THE PERSON, THE MISSION, AND THE LEGACY

BARBOUR
PUBLISHING

To the Rena and Anthony Austin family of Alton, Illinois.

CONTENTS

INTRODUCTION

Perhaps you're already familiar with the life and work of Mother Teresa. Or maybe this book will be a first introduction to the person, the mission, and the legacy. Whatever your starting point, you will no doubt come away with an appreciation for this twentieth-century Roman Catholic nun, one of a group of people we call the Illuminators—faithful believers who carried the light of Jesus Christ to their world.

Mother Teresa is best known for her work with poverty-stricken people in Calcutta, India. But she was also a deeply committed Christian who tried to apply biblical principles to all of society. In this book, you'll read a novelized biography that touches on these major themes of her life. The story casts light on the beliefs and values that made Mother Teresa a force for good, challenging us in the twenty-first century to "go and do likewise" (Luke 10:37).

To Find Hope also provides thought-provoking insights from Mother Teresa's public speeches, which have been lightly edited for easier reading—excerpts from her acceptance speech for a Nobel Peace Prize in 1979 and an address given at the National Prayer Breakfast in Washington, D.C., in 1994.

It is our hope that you'll be inspired by Mother Teresa's example and challenged to live a life that pleases God and benefits humanity.

THE EDITORS

1

NO STRANGER TURNED AWAY

Laughter! Singing! Mandolins!

Two-year-old Gonxha (Gone´-jah) crept out of her bedroom, drawn by the sounds of joy. She wiped sleep from her eyes. Yes. Men danced in the courtyard. There was Papa, dark eyes gleaming above his thick black mustache. His fez tipped dangerously to the side of his head. What was happening?

Gonxha's brother, Lazar, had crept out to watch, too. Some of the men were building something out of small boxes. They looked like the small boxes Mama told her never, never to play with. The men piled them higher and higher. The shouting and laughter were so loud that Gonxha's ears hurt.

"Free at last!" screamed Papa. "Light the torch of liberty!"

Several men lit matches and bent to touch the base of the mountain of small boxes. Tiny flames sprouted. Fire slowly rimmed the base of the mountain. Flames danced up the side of the mountain. Faster and faster. Higher and higher. Dark figures danced around the inferno. The colossal torch shot up into the black sky. Surely the whole world would burn!

"Fire!" screamed Gonxha.

Suddenly, she felt arms enveloping her. "Nothing to fear, my little flower bud. It's only a celebration." It was Mama. "It's like a feast day. But this is for the freedom of Albania!"

Her older sister, Agatha, took her hand. "You've seen enough. Come back to bed with me, naughty girl."

Many months later, however, Gonxha saw despair in her Papa, who some called Nikolai. The celebration where they lit a pile of matchboxes had been held too soon, he grumbled. Yes, Albania had won its independence. But its new territory did not include Skopje, where they lived, or Prizren, where Papa and Mama had once lived. Skopje and Prizren were cities in an area that belonged to the Serbs. But that didn't stop Papa. He still talked about free Albania.

Albania. All that the grown-ups of Gonxha's family, the Bojaxhius (Boy´-ah-gees), seemed to talk about was Albania. Papa and Mama said they were Albanians. At home they spoke Albanian. The priest in the Catholic Church of the Sacred Heart just down the street spoke Albanian. Visitors to the home spoke Albanian. But they didn't live in Albania. They lived in Skopje.

Out on the street, people spoke Turkish and Serbo-Croatian. Only a few spoke Albanian. Of those few speaking Albanian, most were not Catholics like the Bojaxhius but Eastern Orthodox Christians. And many were neither. The low red-tiled skyline of Skopje featured billowing domes of mosques and towering minarets. Many times a day, a man came out on the balcony of the minaret and reminded people to pray. Agatha said it happened five times a day.

"Muslims," said Mama without explaining. It all seemed too complicated.

Except for politics, life at home was very stable, even

though Papa traveled. He was in business with an Italian man named Morten. They bought and sold foodstuffs, fabric, and leather goods. Papa traveled as far away as Italy and Egypt. Every few weeks he would return from a trip with a wagonload of goods he had purchased. These he would sell in Skopje, except of course for the presents he brought back for Mama and the children.

Papa and Mama were very hospitable. They sang and played instruments to entertain guests. Gonxha had to sing, too. She had sung so long beside her brother, Lazar, and sister, Agatha, that singing was as natural to her as it was to a bird.

Her parents' hospitality was not just for evenings. It was offered twenty-four hours a day. Almost every meal had one or more guests. Very often Gonxha had never seen their guests before.

Sometimes she would ask, "Who are these strangers?"

Mama would answer, "Relatives" or "They are our people."

Sometimes their guests were not talkative. Sometimes they were dirty and smelly. Gonxha learned very early that such issues made no difference to Mama. Besides, such smells were nothing compared to what Gonxha saw on visits away from the house she made with Mama. Very often they visited men and women who had to be cleaned before they were fed. Some smelled of wine. Some were covered with nasty sores. One woman they visited very often. Her name was File. She was a drunk, abandoned

There is so much suffering, so much hatred, so much misery, and we with our prayer, with our sacrifice are beginning at home. Love begins at home, and it is not how much we do, but how much love we put in the action that we do.

by her family. Every time Mama and Gonxha visited her, they cleaned her and fed her.

"Jesus was covered with wounds like this, Gonxha," said Mama. "When you help people like this, it's just like helping Jesus."

File was one of many they helped. It was some time before Gonxha could look at the pus and blood in their sores without turning away. Lazar and Agatha could not help such people without getting sick themselves. Eventually Gonxha did see that helping such people was like helping Jesus, just as Mama said. That changed her resolve not to get sick into a great affection for such poor people. Who would not want to help Jesus by helping these sick people?

Once Gonxha was too proud of helping someone. "We had her on her feet in no time," she said breezily to Lazar. "It was like a little miracle, almost like a resurrection."

"Silence!" cried Mama. "When you help such people, you should make no more noise about it than a pebble's tiny splash in the ocean."

Later Mama took her aside and soothed her "little flower bud," which was what Gonxha meant in Albanian. It seemed doubly meaningful to Gonxha that Mama's name, Dranafile, meant "rose" in Albanian.

In the evening, the whole family said prayers together. Then Gonxha was to think very hard on the mystery of Jesus. Sometimes she would think of the joy that came because Jesus came to earth as a baby. Other times she would feel sorrow for His crucifixion. And then there were times when she would think about the glory of Jesus' resurrection.

"Why are you weeping?" Lazar asked Gonxha before bed one evening.

"The crucifixion," she answered, surprised that Lazar was not grieving over the same thing.

When Gonxha was six, she began school at the Church of the Sacred Heart not far away on the very Vlaska Street where they lived. The church seemed like a second home because Mama had taken the three children there for services every morning of their lives. School was run by Father Toma Glasnovic. The first three years were taught in Albanian. In the fourth year, Serbo-Croatian was introduced so the children would be prepared to attend the state-run schools. Learning another language was no problem for the Bojaxhiu children, who heard

Albanian, Serbo-Croatian, Turkish, French, and Italian spoken by Papa.

"There is no *x* in the Serbo-Croatian alphabet," puzzled Gonxha one day.

"Good," snapped Papa. "Your own name—Gonxha Bojaxhiu—will remind you that you are Albanian!"

Soon Gonxha was counting in Serbo-Croatian: "*Yedan, dva, tri, cetiri, pet, sest. . .*"

All three Bojaxhiu children were good students. The smartest was Agatha. The most poetic was Gonxha, who wrote poems and stories. The most interested in the outside world was Lazar, who could scarcely wait to travel like Papa.

But travel was risky now with the war going on. War seemed constant around the area where they lived, but Papa said that now the war had spread all over Europe. It was so vast it was called the Great War. Papa said it had been started by a Serbian. The Serbs, and Albania, too, fought against the Central Powers of Germany, Austria-Hungary, Bulgaria, and their very old enemy, Turkey.

The Great War was simply a continuation of war for Albanians. They had battled for two years before that in what some called the Balkan Wars.

"Perhaps someday I will fight for Albania," Lazar told Papa.

Each summer the whole family journeyed northwest up out of the valley of the Vardar River on to Cerna Gora, or Black Mountain. Their horse-drawn coach passed peasants wearing white shirts and colorful vests, who were herding sheep and cattle. The boys carried staffs for prodding stubborn animals. The bearded men wore fur pillbox hats and knee-high boots even in summer. The trail echoed with rattling wheels of small carts pulled by donkeys and large wagons pulled by oxen.

"Where are they going?" asked Gonxha.

"Don't you see?" said Agatha. "When they go the same way we go, they are empty. When they go back down into Skopje, they are full of lambs and vegetables and eggs and all sorts of things to eat."

"I thought Papa brought in the food we ate."

"Papa only brings in special things to eat. From far-away places."

Looking back down into the Vardar Valley, Gonxha saw only red-tiled roofs broken by the minarets. She didn't ask why there were no high cupolas of Christian churches. She knew by now that the Turks had forbidden it.

She also knew the great stone bridge—the Kameni

Most—in Skopje across the Vardar was built by Romans. And of course Jesus lived during the time the Romans ruled. Gonxha saw the road that went south from Skopje to Katlanovska. The Bojaxhiu family took that road occasionally to bathe in hot springs. Papa said if one continued farther to the south, the road went into Greece, right to Salonika, the apostle Paul's Thessalonica! Not far east of there was Philippi, now called Kavalla.

Gonxha nudged Agatha. "What happened at Philippi?"

"The apostle Paul established the first Christian church in Europe."

"What else?"

"Alexander the Great lived there long before Jesus was born. Later Caesar Augustus caught Brutus and Cassius there."

"The killers of Julius Caesar?"

"Yes."

How could Gonxha not feel as if she were in the mainstream of history? And God was the Master of history. The Greeks, the Romans, the earliest Christians, the great Serbian kings, the Turks. It was wonderful to think of all that had happened so close to her own home.

The stout horses pulling the Bojaxhiu family coach soon clopped along mountain trails to the shrine of the Madonna of Cernagore at Letnica. The shrine was in a monastery. The mountains around Skopje were full of Christian monasteries, said Papa, many built by the great Serbian king Milutin five hundred years before. Then the Turks came, he scowled. But his face would quickly brighten. After all, now the Turks were vanquished. He was careful to explain that the battle was not religious. Most of their Albanian brothers were Muslims. It was an ethnic battle that people outside the Balkans would never understand.

"Politics," sighed Mama. Her voice carried toleration but no sympathy.

The large single cupola Gonxha saw was typical of the monasteries in the area around Skopje. So, too, was emphasizing the form of the structure by alternating bricks and native stone. Different levels inside the monastery honored saints, Serbian kings, apostles, and Jesus. Near the entrance was a statue of the Virgin Mary and the baby Jesus.

When the Bojaxhius visited the shrine high on Black Mountain, they stayed in the house of Papa's friend. Papa had helped build it. There the family became even closer, away from the everyday demands of Skopje. Every waking hour was devoted to worship and family. They sang, told stories, played games, and went for walks.

"Now don't bury your head in a book every moment, Gonxha," scolded Mama. "Get some exercise." Mama worried because her youngest child often coughed.

By this time Gonxha realized that her family was wealthy. When Papa became a city councilman, she realized her family had influence, too. Their life was very rich by all accounts. Priests, even dignitaries of the church, came to their home to eat with them.

"God bless you, Nikolai, for your kindness," they would say. Apparently Papa gave very generously to the church. It seemed like their very rich life would last forever.

"For I was hungry and you gave me something to eat, I was thirsty and you gave me something to drink, I was a stranger and you invited me in, I needed clothes and you clothed me, I was sick and you looked after me, I was in prison and you came to visit me."

MATTHEW 25:35–36

2

HOPE IN CHRIST

Lazar!" Gonxha couldn't believe her tall, twelve-year-old brother was in the kitchen helping himself to candy.

Lazar spun to face his much smaller sister of eight. "Gonxha, be quiet," he hissed.

"No," Gonxha replied. "You shouldn't be eating after midnight."

"Don't be such a stickler. Do you really think God cares if I eat a chocolate?"

"You cannot eat after midnight and go to church in the morning. You cannot take Holy Communion."

Lazar studied his younger sister carefully before answering. It was too dark in the kitchen to see how serious she was. "It's not midnight yet." He popped a chocolate in his mouth.

"I heard the chimes of the hall clock. It is later than midnight."

He popped another chocolate in his mouth. "Tell Mother, then."

"Even a child is known by his doings, whether his work be pure, and whether it be right," Gonxha quoted from Proverbs.

"Not unless you tell."

"God knows."

"Go to bed, Gonxha."

Gonxha returned to the bedroom where she slept with Agatha. Agatha might have said to Lazar just what Gonxha said to him. But Agatha was fifteen now and a heavy sleeper. What would Mama have said? What would Papa have said? Probably what Gonxha had said. But Mama would have refused to take him to church. Papa, who was out of town, would have strapped him.

But didn't it all amount to the same thing? Lazar had disobeyed God. Gonxha was taught in her church not to eat from midnight until after Sunday morning's early church service, where communion was taken.

The next morning the Bojaxhiu family (except for Papa, who had not yet returned from his trip) walked to church. It had rained in the night. October rain made the air heavy with chill. Lazar acted as if nothing was wrong. That bothered Gonxha, but she had known for a long time that guilt could not be read on the face of most guilty people.

So how would one know if a neighbor was guilty? An uncle? An aunt? Only God knew. The only exception Gonxha knew was Mama, whom all three children now called *Nana loke*, or "Mother of my soul." Mama wore guilt like a rash—not that she had many times to feel guilty about anything.

When they arrived at the Church of the Sacred Heart, Gonxha and her sister flew off to join the choir. Agatha often sang contralto in groups, and some whispered that Gonxha was going to sing even more beautifully. As a soprano, she would solo. *God forgive me for remembering such praise*, Gonxha thought.

During the church service, Gonxha's heart ached as she watched Lazar take Holy Communion. How was one to weigh one sin against another? Perhaps that was what Jesus meant about not judging. Judgment was His. Still, the parent must teach the child. But what were the duties of the child? And why did none of her friends ever worry about such troublesome things?

Walking home, Gonxha asked Mama, "Where is Papa?" This trip had seemed different because a look of worry often crossed Mama's face.

"He's in Belgrade."

"Buying textiles?"

"No. It's a political meeting. They are discussing bringing the area around Prizren into Albania."

Politics. Gonxha asked no more questions. It seemed that after the Great War ended, their city of Skopje was no longer part of Serbia. It had become part of a very large country called Yugoslavia. Now father worked with others to get the area around Prizren included in the country of Albania instead of Yugoslavia. Papa didn't even live in Prizren anymore, but he'd never lost his love or concern for his hometown. Most people in that area spoke Albanian. It seemed logical enough for someone who lived there to want to be part of the country of Albania, but Mama was worried about it.

That evening Papa came home from Belgrade very ill. He had to be helped out of the carriage by his friends. Gonxha had never seen his handsome tan face so pale. His eyes were glazed. He didn't even recognize her.

"Something he ate, no doubt," said Lazar in a worried tone.

Mother put Papa to bed and shooed the children away. Gonxha prayed. She had seen too many sick people not to know Papa was extremely sick. She said nothing to the other two. She had learned to keep worrisome things inside her. Only God could help Papa. So she prayed and prayed.

MOTHER TERESA ON CHRIST'S LOVE:

[Jesus] died on the cross to show a greater love, and he died for you and for me and for that leper and for that man dying of hunger and that naked person lying in the street not only of Calcutta, but of Africa, and New York, and London, and Oslo.

Then the most wrenching thing imaginable happened. Gonxha could only stare as Mama entered the room. Blood stained the front of Mama's dress.

"Little flower bud," said Mama. "Go get the priest."

God, help us, Gonxha prayed silently as she rushed out onto the street and stumbled toward the church. She could scarcely think. In a daze, she lurched inside the building. The curate saw her. Quickly Gonxha explained her mission.

"No, the Father is not here," the curate said. "He might be arriving soon at the railway station."

Gonxha walked quickly back out onto the street and raced all the way across the old Roman bridge over the Vardar River to the railway station. There on the platform she found not her parish priest, but a priest she did not know.

She never hesitated. "You must come, Father. My

papa may be on his deathbed."

"Of course, child."

Gonxha hurriedly led the priest back to their home on Vlaska Street.

"Hemorrhaging, Father," Gonxha heard Mama tell the priest. Papa was pale and sweaty. Was he conscious? Gonxha couldn't tell.

The priest began, *"Asperges me, Domine, hyssopo, et mundabor; lavabis me, et super nivem dealbabor. . ."*

Mama made Gonxha leave and stay in her bedroom. If Papa was conscious, he would confess to the priest. It must be in private. The priest was still speaking Latin as Gonxha left. The words of Psalm 51 were so comforting. "Purge me, oh Lord, with hyssop and I shall be clean: wash me, and I shall be whiter than snow."

Gonxha often forgot she knew Latin. It was as second nature to her as was Albanian. Latin united Catholics all over the world. One could be in Tierra del Fuego at the southern tip of the world, or in the Belgian Congo, or in the stormy ice fields of Greenland in the far north and still understand any Catholic priest because they used Latin. It reminded them that Christ transcended all customs, all languages.

As soon as Gonxha got to her bedroom, she fell on her knees and prayed. She knew the priest would give Papa "last anointing." After quoting from Psalm 51, he would say several prayers beseeching the help of God and His angels. If Papa was conscious, he would have a chance for a last confession. Then, with his thumb, the priest would anoint Papa with oil. The priest would also say a prayer asking forgiveness of Papa's sins.

It was all too awful to think about. And yet what greater solace was there than the hope of Christ? In spite of herself, sometime in the night she fell asleep. The next morning, Gonxha learned Papa was in the hospital.

"So there is hope!" she cried.

"There is always hope in Christ," replied Mama. But Mama wasn't smiling.

Gonxha knew the outlook for Papa must be very poor. Even so, when he died the following day, Gonxha was stunned. And for the first time Gonxha could remember, Mama seemed numb herself. The funeral service was attended by a crowd so large, the family could barely squeeze through. Many shops in Skopje were closed.

As tradition required, the family distributed commemorative handkerchiefs to friends and acquaintances throughout the city. Their wealth permitted them to send out hundreds. Perhaps more than a thousand handkerchiefs, Gonxha heard someone say. Every schoolchild in Skopje received one.

Mama seemed more in control now. "Papa is with God sooner," she whispered to Gonxha.

Afterward Gonxha heard many kind stories about Papa. His reputation was even greater than she had thought. He was only forty-five, but he had done so much for Skopje. He had been an excellent pharmacist at one time. As a building contractor he had helped build the city's first theater. He played in a band called the Voice of the Mountains. He helped some band members buy their instruments. He gave a lot of money to the church. Even the archbishop Lazar Mjeda thanked him and had stayed in their home.

Lazar admitted running many errands of mercy for Papa, delivering packages to the poor. Papa gave out money, food, and clothing. Many of the poor who came to the Bojaxhius's dinner table had been invited by Papa.

The Albanian patriots Hasan Prishtina and Sabri Qytezi knew Papa. He had also known Curri, the great fighter against the Turks. In fact, the three men had stayed in their home. Gonxha had been too young to realize all the fine things about Papa. So, although it was painful to talk about him, it was also wonderful to hear all the things about him that she hadn't known.

Gonxha had her own memories of him. "Never take a bite of food that you are not willing to share with others, my daughter," he had told her. He was tough, too. "Always remember whose children you are!" he would instruct Gonxha and her brother and sister.

Papa's mischievous son, Lazar, had concerned him most. Sometimes Papa would wake Lazar up at night to ask him if he had been good at school that day. He trusted Agatha most, just as Mama trusted Gonxha in spite of her youth. After all, who had she sent for the priest? Gonxha, a mere eight years old. . .

"Forgive me, God, for thinking that," prayed Gonxha. Why had she spoiled her wonderful memories by praising herself? Hadn't she been taught to always be on guard against Satan's temptations?

One day she overheard a conversation that tore at her heart. Some Albanians thought Papa had been poisoned. To poison poor Papa just because he wanted an area for ethnic Albanians to be in the country of Albania? It was very hard not to be bitter about such an injustice. But Gonxha knew she must forgive those who might have done it so that she could keep Papa's memory noble and kind.

From that time on, however, Gonxha recognized the dangers of politics. She understood why members of religious orders were not political. To be political, a person took one side of an argument and opposed people on the other side. Christ said to love all your neighbors—and your enemies, too. The religious were only on the side of God. The more Gonxha learned about life, the more perfect Christianity seemed to her. And who set a better example for her of how to live a Christian life than the priests and nuns of her church?

In the meantime Mama coped with her grief. How Mama had loved Papa. Every day before he was expected home, she had put on a clean dress and primped herself. She had often told Gonxha, "Ask me for anything, and I'll try to give it to you—but I expect something in return." In return for Papa's love, she had given him the very best she had to offer.

"How she will miss him!" said Lazar.

"As we all will," added Agatha.

Still, the Bojaxhiu family could not grieve forever. In spite of her pain, Mama had to evaluate the family's finances. It seemed Papa had trusted his partner Morten too well. The Bojaxhiu family could draw on some assets for a while, but soon only the house itself would be left. Mama would have to find a way to make a living. She wouldn't consider for a moment letting any of the children work to help meet their financial needs.

"You must complete your schooling," she told them. "The world is too hard without an education."

So to the utter amazement of Gonxha, Mama went into business. She began by dealing with handcrafted embroidery. Then she also began dealing in the carpets for which Skopje was so well known.

At first the doors of manufacturers were opened to her because of the owners' affection for Papa. But it was soon clear to these businessmen that Mama was quite capable. Lazar often went with her to deliver or pick up carpets.

"They ask Mama's advice on which designs will sell," he told Agatha and Gonxha in amazement. "And she tells them!"

"Don't you know Mama's parents in Prizren were merchants?" Agatha asked him. "How could Mama not know how to conduct business? It was just that she had not been required to do so for so many years."

This conversation taught Gonxha a very valuable lesson. Every person is usually far more gifted than other people realize. Far more valuable.

"And the poor we help?" she asked herself. "Yes, they, too, are valuable. For material wealth means nothing in God's eyes."

Mama still had a strong hold on the children. She was not too tired to manage the home. One evening the three children were chattering away in the living room. The conversation became sillier and sillier. Even Gonxha, so serious most of the time, got carried away. Mama quietly rose from her chair and left the room. Suddenly, the house was dark.

From the blackness Mama yelled, "I turned off the electricity. I won't waste such a good thing on such foolishness!"

During those years, Gonxha often wondered what she would become when she got older. Would she marry like Mama? She was doing very well in her first years in the state-run school. Would she continue on into college and study economics as Agatha planned? Gonxha certainly couldn't go to a military academy as Lazar planned to do! She liked to write poetry. But one couldn't make a living that way. Perhaps she could write stories for a newspaper.

"Or perhaps I could become a teacher," she mused.

At about this time, a major change happened in

Gonxha's church. For some time, church members had known they needed some additional outside help to get all the things that needed to be done taken care of. In 1921, three years after the Great War ended, their church was turned over to the Jesuits, an order in the Catholic Church known for its teaching.

When Gonxha learned the news, she thought that perhaps the new priest, Father Gaspar Zadrima, would give her some advice about teaching. He was an Albanian, fluent in Serbo-Croatian, too, so the Bojaxhiu children immediately felt comfortable with him. But he could be very stern with children who weren't obedient or disciplined.

"How can anyone like someone who carries an enormous stick?" complained Lazar. "And he uses it, too."

"It is your duty to love him and respect him," countered Gonxha. "He is one of Christ's priests."

"You are so obedient," shot back Lazar in a mocking voice. "You should be a nun. Chastity, poverty, obedience."

"We are not poor," she answered.

Lazar groaned. "How did I get into such a family of saints?" Yet his voice carried no anger. How could it? After all, his little sister usually did his chores for him.

Father Zadrima did not forget Gonxha's first timid questions about teaching. The following year, another priest arrived to assist him, but although the priest was eager to help, he couldn't speak Albanian fluently. He found it very difficult to teach catechism to the Albanian-speaking children.

One day Father Zadrima called in Gonxha and explained the problem.

"But I have the perfect solution," said Father Zadrima.

"Prayer?" asked Gonxha.

"Yes. And my prayer has been answered. God sent me a young girl with a wide forehead full of knowledge and large brown eyes full of a desire to teach."

From then on Gonxha interpreted for Father Zadrima's assistant. It wasn't long before she felt she could teach the catechism herself. Of course, she couldn't answer questions as easily and as accurately as the priest could. But for a twelve-year-old girl, she possessed a great deal of knowledge about the church. This gave her a new idea, which she shared with her mother.

"Mama, I am thinking of a life in the service of the church."

Mama was used to the dreams of twelve-year-old children and knew that they often changed over the years. "You have much time yet to decide, little flower bud," she said calmly. "Continue your education and learn as much as you can."

Gonxha followed her mama's advice, and for the next two years, life in their family was surprisingly calm. But then in 1923, sixteen-year-old Lazar left home. He had received a scholarship to study in Austria for a year. When he returned home, he seemed certain to get an appointment at the military academy in the capital of Albania. It seemed Lazar had left the home for good.

"How sad," Gonxha confided to her mother one day.

"Nothing is forever, little flower bud," Mama reminded her.

Gonxha continued her life of state education and church activities. In school she became a top student. Any class photograph showed the very serious Gonxha, with wide, high forehead and luminous eyes. Her large, open face looked more like a teacher's face than a student's. She worked at home, doing Lazar's old chores as well as her own. She visited the poor with Mama. She sang duets with Agatha at church functions. In her spare moments, she played with friends, read books, and composed poems.

Gonxha was fourteen when Father Zadrima was replaced by another Jesuit, Father Franjo Jambrekovich. Each priest brought something new to the church. Father

Jambrekovich introduced more activities in the church for boys and girls. They held parties, outings, walks, and meetings. Gonxha even learned to play the mandolin from one of the boys. And there was a much more serious group for girls only. It was called a sodality.

Father Jambrekovich told the girls, "Remember Saint Ignatius Loyola's words, my children: 'What have I done for Christ? What *am* I doing for Christ? What *will* I do for Christ?'"

"The church has started a sodality," Gonxha told Mama with enthusiasm.

And the sodality became the focus of Gonxha's energy.

> Then I heard the voice of the Lord saying,
> "Whom shall I send? And who will go for us?"
> And I said, "Here am I. Send me!"
> ISAIAH 6:8

3

GOD'S CALL

Gonxha couldn't get her fill of activities in the sodality. She volunteered for everything. One time she even reported to her sisters about recent mission activity around the world.

Father Jambrekovich praised her. "Pope Benedict XV started a push for more missions ten years ago," he explained. "And now Pius XI is pushing mission activity even harder. Some of our own Jesuits are now in India. Yugoslavians like us, too. Read their letters in *Catholic Missions*, Gonxha."

Gonxha became fascinated with stories of India. How large it was! The land. The many languages and religions. The number of people. The suffering. Soon the sounds of India slipped off her tongue as easily as if they had been there since birth. Darjeeling. Bengal. The Sunderbans. Calcutta. Ganges. It was overwhelming. She began to read everything she could find on India.

Of course she learned about India's politics. The great
empire of Britain controlled India. The British had steadily
increased their influence over India since the 1600s. They
had even created the mighty city of Calcutta out of a tiny
river town. But in the late 1800s, educated Hindus began
to organize a nationalist movement. The most powerful
was the Indian National Congress. Violence against British
rule became more and more frequent, particularly in Bengal, the very area most appealing to Gonxha.

Political intrigue increased when the British encouraged the formation of the Muslim League. This would
split the effort for independence into Hindus and Muslims, reasoned the British. And what better result than to
have the two factions fight each other instead of Britain?

After the Great War, one person emerged who might

be able to unite Hindus and Muslims: Mohandas K. Gandhi. Gandhi, a lawyer educated in London, advocated *swaraj*, or India for the Indians. He wore nothing but a *dhoti*, traditional Indian clothing that looked like a diaper to cynical westerners. He advocated simple native diets and cottage industries. He was scrupulously honest. Many Indians regarded him as holy.

"Gandhi is the man the British truly fear," reasoned Gonxha as she studied.

Although Gandhi worked for peaceful resistance, many of his followers stormed out of control. Riots ended in bloodshed. But the most savage brutality was by the British against the Indians. None signaled British resistance to Indian freedom more than what happened at Amritsar in 1919. British troops opened fire on a crowd of demonstrators, killing 379 people.

Six years later, as Gonxha read everything she could find about India, Gandhi languished in prison. What would happen if he were free, Gonxha wondered. Could the British withstand hundreds of millions of Indians if they ever united in a rebellion? And could Gandhi control their passions? Would they slaughter every white face, she wondered, suddenly aware of her pale skin.

But India had many dangers besides violent politics. Malaria and tuberculosis and starvation were common. Not to mention elephants, tigers, and cobras. What would a small girl like her do there? And she didn't mean young, she meant small. At fifteen years old, it was obvious that Gonxha would never be taller than five feet. And it seemed impossible that she would ever weigh as much as one hundred pounds. Still, Gonxha figured, if she couldn't go to India, she could serve the church in some other way. But was God calling her? She talked to Mama.

"You seem uncertain. That is a warning, little flower bud," said Mama. "Still, if you begin it, you must do it with all your heart and soul! Otherwise, don't do it."

Gonxha suspected Mama did not want her to make such a sacrifice. Agatha and Gonxha's girlfriends knew about her longings, too. They were little help. Agatha wanted to be an economist. To be a Christian was one thing, but to dedicate every waking minute to Christ was quite another!

"Why don't you write for a newspaper?" asked Agatha.

The other girls agreed. "The local paper has printed several of Gonxha's submissions on the sodality and the missions," they said.

Lazar had already told Gonxha that such a rigid religious life was a life wasted for a young person full of energy and ambition. Finally Gonxha went to Father Jambrekovich for advice.

"How can I know if God is calling me to serve the church?" she asked. "And if I am called to serve, how do I know what He wants me to do?"

"Joy," the priest answered without hesitation. "Joy will spring out of your heart when you think on it. Joy is a compass. Even if the road you think about is very difficult, joy will tell you if that is your path."

Gonxha walked away from the meeting, pleased at first, then puzzled. What gave her joy?

But by the time Gonxha turned sixteen, she was certain. Every time she thought of serving Christ, joy sprang from her heart. But how would she serve? Joy was her compass there, too. Nothing gave her more joy than thinking about being a missionary. And nothing gave her more joy than thinking about serving Christ in India.

Other questions now filled Gonxha's mind. How could a nun become a missionary and reach India? What if she got something started that she couldn't stop? For two years, Gonxha agonized over her future.

"It's high time to find out," she told herself at last.

She had read dozens of letters from India written by Yugoslav priests. She knew that those priests served beside the sisters of the Institute of the Blessed Virgin Mary. That was an order of nuns that Gonxha knew nothing about. Gonxha's research soon revealed that some of the nuns were also called the sisters of Loreto. They were teachers, just as Gonxha wanted to be.

"But their order serves India from Ireland," she explained to her sister, Agatha.

"Then you must go to Ireland, I suppose," shrugged Agatha.

So Agatha did not think it was farfetched. What would Mama think? Gonxha went to her.

Mama was stunned. Ireland? India? Didn't Gonxha

know nuns did not get vacations? Nuns did not travel about. They took a vow of poverty. Didn't Gonxha realize a mission as far away as India meant she would be permanently separated from her family? Mama would never see her little flower bud again!

Mama stumbled into her bedroom looking as stricken as she had the day Papa had died. She did not come out of her bedroom for twenty-four hours. When she appeared the next day, she was looking very drained.

"Well, little flower bud," Mama told Gonxha sadly, "you may leave with my blessing. But please strive to live only for God and Christ!"

Gonxha and Lazar exchanged letters. He protested as never before. "Don't you know you are going to bury yourself alive in the middle of nowhere?" he wrote angrily.

Gonxha was angry, too, and it showed in the reply she sent to her brother. "I suppose you think you are important because you serve your King Zog and two million Albanians? Well, I'm serving the King of the whole world!"

Lazar was not alone. Many comments about Gonxha's decision stung her. How poorly the world understood people who decided to devote themselves to the church. Well-meaning relatives and friends said the most ignorant things about nuns. "Surely the poor nuns want desperately to get out of the convent," they protested. "Once they take their vows, the poor nuns can never get out. It must be awful to be trapped inside the convent. Oh, what a terrible sacrifice they must bear. How can

MOTHER TERESA ON HER WORK:

I believe that we are not real social workers. We may be doing social work in the eyes of the people, but we are really contemplatives in the heart of the world. For we are touching the body of Christ twenty-four hours a day.

they pass up a life of marriage? How can they pass up a life of pleasure?"

Gonxha knew those things were not true. The nuns she saw were full of joy. But she had to admit she had thought all those ignorant things once herself. When she first thought of becoming a nun when she was twelve, how the doubts had haunted her. So she could not condemn others for thinking the same way. Why not change their thinking by setting an example?

"Why not show what great joy a religious person possesses?" she asked herself.

Despite people's objections, the matter was settled, at least for Gonxha and her family and friends. There was still the matter of being accepted into the order she wanted. How would she go about it? Would she write a letter? And would they understand Serbo-Croatian? Or Albanian? She asked Father Jambrekovich.

"I'll talk to my Jesuit brothers." He added thoughtfully,

"What young lady has served the church more faithfully than Gonxha Bojaxhiu?"

"Thank you," she said, somewhat puzzled.

Days dragged by as she waited for an answer. Was the process so mysterious? So slow? Had Father Jambrekovich forgotten? Priests were so busy. She began to fret. Life was rolling by. And she hadn't even taken the first step yet. Prayer soothed her fear. If the process was slow or nonexistent, then God had a reason. But it was so hard to wait.

Meanwhile, she learned the Irish branch of the Institute of the Blessed Virgin Mary had only been there since 1822. The order was actually founded in Holland in 1609 by Mary Ward, an Englishwoman who fled Yorkshire. Catholics were persecuted by the very King James I who authorized the famous English translation of the Bible.

Mary Ward used much of the rule of the Jesuits in her charter. Meditate, but act! Teaching and attention to the poor were at the heart of her order. Her intention was for her order not to be confined to the walls of the convent. She wanted the sisters to have the freedom to seek out the poorest of the poor. Her tombstone read: "To love the poore, Persevere in the same, Live, die and rise with them, Was all the ayme of Mary Ward." These words won Gonxha's heart.

"Isn't that much like what dear Mama does?" she asked.

But then Gonxha learned that after Mary Ward's

death, the order had a reversal of fortune. Their freedom to reach the poor outside the convent walls was taken away from them by a pope's decree in 1690. Gonxha learned that the members of the order were still confined to their convents.

"How nice," Gonxha told herself, "that Mary Ward had based her rule of the congregation on the rule of the Jesuits."

After all, Jesuit priests had been Gonxha's spiritual mentors as she grew up. She already knew a lot about Jesuits. The order had been founded in 1540 by Saint Ignatius of Loyola. Ignatius was born a Spanish noble-man in 1491. The family castle was in the Pyrenees Mountains bordering France. His early life was anything but saintly. Besides pursuing romance, he chased adventure as a professional soldier. At the age of thirty, he was seriously wounded in a skirmish against the French. It was during a long recuperation at his ancestral home that he read two religious books: *Flowers of the Saints* and Ludolph of Saxony's *Life of Christ*. His interest was motivated by nothing more than boredom, but the books overwhelmed him. If the ultimate truths were God and Christianity, did it not seem reasonable to pursue them to the limit of his understanding?

Ignatius recovered from his wounds enough to journey to the monastery at Montserrat near Barcelona. Rather than dress in his usual elegant fashions, he wore the ragged clothes of a beggar. At a shrine there he dedicated his life, and then retreated into a cave near Manresa. It was 1522. For ten months, Ignatius prayed and meditated. Influenced by *Exercises for the Spiritual Life* by the abbot Garcia de Cisneros, Ignatius formulated his own Spiritual Exercises in four stages. In the first, one must develop a profound conviction of the folly of sin. In the next stage, one must realize with all one's heart and mind that Christ is active in the world. In the next, one must decide how to collaborate with Christ. To do this, the seeker must use spiritual discernment to choose a vocation. In the last stage, the seeker contemplates rewards from collaboration with Christ, not the least of which is the loving companionship of other seekers.

Over the years Ignatius refined his exercises. "Finding God in all things" was his guide. The hallmark of Jesuit spirituality became meditation, then implementation. Yes, prayer. But then service. Yes, contemplation. But then action. Followers of his order meditated daily. Every day they examined their own faithfulness. They went on retreat annually to perform the Spiritual Exercises. Gonxha learned that Ignatius's Spiritual Exercises still formed the model for most Roman Catholic missions and retreats.

"And one of Ignatius's contemporary Jesuits was none other than Saint Francis of Xavier," enthused Gonxha. "And where did this great Jesuit soldier go? India, of course!"

Gonxha was amazed how everything seemed to tie together for her own vocation. Yet she waited. Week after week. Finally Father Jambrekovich called for her. Her mind was spinning with doubt as she walked toward his office. Never had she imagined that the process would take so long. She walked into his office and sat down nervously.

"Won't I have to write a letter of application, Father?" she blurted out. "Won't I need to send letters of recommendation? Don't I need my certificate of baptism? Of confirmation? Shouldn't I have asked for these documents already?"

"Calm yourself, child." He smiled. "You need not write anything. One of the brothers spoke to the mother superior of the sisters of Loreto in Paris."

"Paris? But—"

"She will interview you for the mother general in Ireland."

How could she have doubted? The days whirled by. On August 15, 1928, during the feast of the Assumption of the Virgin, Gonxha went one last time to the shrine of the Madonna of Letnica on Black Mountain. She prayed for God's blessing on her decision. She had been there often the past two years. Surely this direction she was taking was the right one.

During Gonxha's final week in Skopje, the church marked her departure with a solemn paschal feast. But on September 25, her sodality, the choir, and members of the youth group gathered at her house for a farewell celebration. They gave her gifts. The next morning they were at the railway station to say good-bye. Their faces

MOTHER TERESA ON THE POOR:

The poor are very great people. They can teach us so many beautiful things. These poor people maybe have nothing to eat, maybe they have not a home to live in, but they can still be great people when they are spiritually rich.

now seemed stunned. Gonxha knew they were wondering what would happen to their tiny friend in far-off India.

"God be with you always," she said as she stepped onto the train.

Gonxha had resolved not to cry. But tears streamed down her cheeks as she looked out through the window of the train. The train lurched, then gathered speed toward its destination of Zagreb. The parting was sad but not unbearable, because Mama and Agatha were still with her.

Gonxha let herself thrill at the beauty of Yugoslavia as the train shot north, skirting mountains, then entered the long green valley of the Sava. In Zagreb they left the train to wait for Betike Kanjc, who also wanted to become a sister of Loreto. Gonxha was numb. An awful moment was approaching. And finally it came. Betike arrived. Gonxha had to watch Mama and Agatha, standing on the platform, vanish into the distance as her train sped toward Paris. Would she ever see them again?

"It's very hard," consoled Betike.

The train bolted north across Slovenia toward Vienna. Once in the valley of the Danube River, it rolled west across Austria, then into Germany, and finally through France. The Danube River was now far behind them. It seemed impossible to Gonxha that they were now following the valley of the Seine River. How fast events were moving. Her head was reeling. But the future never frightened her as long as she remembered she was in God's hands.

"Do you speak French?" Gonxha asked Betike timidly.

"No," blurted Betike, surprised by the question. Worry flickered across her face.

In Paris, at the great railway station on the east side of the city, the two young ladies were met by a priest. They were whisked away by a chattering automobile. They soon realized their great fortune. The mother superior must have been on the west side of Paris, for they passed one famous landmark after another. But none compared to the sight of the great gothic cathedral of Notre Dame.

Finally, they arrived in a district of Paris called Auteuil. At the Loreto House, they were introduced to an interpreter from the Yugoslavian embassy. Gonxha had worried poor Betike over nothing. When would she learn to let God open doors for her?

Soon the girls were talking to Mother Superior Eugene MacAvin. What questions could the mother superior ask Gonxha that would thwart her plans? Certainly nothing about the catechism. Most important were Gonxha's sincerity and will to serve Christ. Betike was satisfactory, too, because soon both young ladies were being driven to a railway station on the west side of Paris. All apprehension evaporated. Within hours they were on a ship headed to Ireland.

"One, two, three," said Gonxha in English, while looking in a book.

"Molim?" asked Betike in Serbo-Croatian, meaning, "Pardon me?"

"Yedan, dva, tri," answered Gonxha in Serbo-Croatian, laughing.

The interpreter had given them books so they could study English during the rest of their journey. The stay in Ireland would be short. No formal novitiate training would occur. They were not even novices. They were postulants, a stage that prepared them for the novitiate. They would spend almost every moment learning English. Once in India as novices they would be formally taught the novitiate in English for at least one year. It would become their first language.

The process seemed strange to Gonxha. She knew some novices changed their minds before they took their vows. But how could she change her mind if she were already in India?

At Loreto Abbey near Dublin, the two postulants from Yugoslavia were put in the hands of Mother M. Borgia Irwin. She had been to India. And she would teach them English. They saw little of other novices and postulants. The two quickly understood they would soon be on their way. There was no time to waste. When the ship sailed for India in the middle of November, they would be on it!

In a letter from Skopje, Gonxha learned what had been written about her in *Catholic Missions*:

> *Just as Saint Peter immediately left his nets behind him, so Gonxha left her books and set off in the name of God. Everyone was surprised, because she was top of her class and much admired. She was the life and soul of the Catholic girls' activities and the church choir, and it was generally acknowledged that her departure would leave an enormous gap. When she left Skopje, about a hundred people were at the station to see her off. They were all in tears.*[1]

She could scarcely believe her eyes. What a tribute to her, the little flower bud. What had she done? Nothing yet. Oh, she mustn't be so humble as to deceive anyone. She was now wearing a habit, it was true—a simple black dress and black veil. But she was not wearing the white stiff coif under the veil because she was not yet a novice. She was almost a postulant. Sort of. And one day she noticed a discernment in the eyes of Mother M. Borgia Irwin that startled her.

Gonxha could almost hear the pious woman wondering: *Can Gonxha Bojaxhiu handle the work? Does she work hard? Can she handle pressure? Does she pout? Does she slip off to weep? Does she lapse into melancholy? Does she ever, God forbid, fly into a rage? Does she hold grudges? Is she stubborn? Is she opinionated? Does she magnify her faults? Does she underestimate her faults? Does she associate with everyone? Is she pleasant to everyone?*

Oh yes, the eyes of Gonxha's English teacher told her that the two girls from Yugoslavia had not yet earned a trip to India. How could Gonxha have been so naive as to think she was in Ireland merely to take English lessons? She wouldn't respect an order that shipped some simple, unstable girl off to faraway lands. She longed to confide in Betike. But something told her to hold her suspicions. By saying something, she might thwart the sisters' intentions.

"Thank You, Lord," Gonxha prayed that night. "Thank You for giving me a mind to discern." Then she tried to say the same prayer in English.

How hard she prayed that she and Betike would go to India!

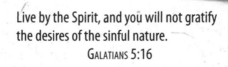

Live by the Spirit, and you will not gratify the desires of the sinful nature.
GALATIANS 5:16

4

CALCUTTA, INDIA

In November 1929, Gonxha and Betike boarded the *Marcha*. Three Franciscan sisters were on board, too. Together the five women organized an active prayer life. They wouldn't be able to celebrate Holy Communion for many weeks because no priest was aboard. But when they sailed into the Mediterranean and anchored at Port Said, the five companions took the opportunity to go ashore and attend services at a local church. Soon the *Marcha* was once again sailing. The ship passed through the Suez Canal into the Red Sea and finally made it to the Indian Ocean.

"Oh, Betike," Gonxha said in the English they continued to practice, "how wonderful it would be to arrive in India on Christmas Day."

"Don't wish us there too quickly, Sister," said a deckhand who overheard her. "We don't want to sail into one of the last monsoon storms of the year."

Although the air smelled of tropical delights, land was not in sight Christmas Day. The five travelers created a nativity scene and sang Christmas carols. As darkness fell, their singing grew more solemn. They sang "Gloria," said prayers, and ended by singing "Adestes Fidelis," which they also had learned to sing in English as "O Come, All Ye Faithful." The final words, "O come, let us adore him, Christ, the Lord," warmed Gonxha's heart.

"Land!" someone yelled two days later.

Gonxha rushed to the ship's rail and strained her eyes. It was some time before the horizon sprouted a dark bluish halo. Then it became a cap of green that kept growing bigger. They were sailing into Colombo, the capital city of the island of Ceylon. To the English who ruled that part of the world, there was scant difference between Ceylon and its giant neighbor, India. Gonxha certainly could not distinguish between the two. She really felt she had arrived in India.

"Welcome, Sisters," said a man who came aboard. "I'm Mr. Scanlon."

The city seemed a lush garden. Tall palms reached into the sky everywhere. It was very hot and humid. But Gonxha ignored the heaviness and breathed in the exotic tropics. The air smelled of spices and sweat. Sounds flooded over them. Tinkling bells, buzzing flies, pounding shoemakers, shouting merchants. Sights overwhelmed them, too: pastries, sacks of grain, sparkling jewelry, enameled boxes, combs, silks, brocades.

The merchants were dark skinned and wore wraps of bright colors. But many men were half naked. Some of these men, called coolies, pulled two-wheeled carts like draft animals. The carts were called rickshaws. Then Mr. Scanlon insisted the five women ride in such carts. How Gonxha wanted to refuse. But it might seem very ungrateful. So all of them rode first to Saint Joseph's Missionary School, then to Mr. Scanlon's house.

At first the *pat, pat, pat* of the coolie's feet pierced Gonxha with guilt. It worsened as he began to pant, then wheeze. Guilt and sadness hammered her with his every gasping breath. Sweat poured from his skin. Was India going to be full of such inhuman customs?

The next day they visited the sisters of the Good Shepherd. By now Gonxha knew Ceylon was not like

India. The people were overwhelmingly Buddhists. Hindus, who made up the majority of people in India, were a small minority in Ceylon, but there were even fewer Christians.

"Betike, look!" cried Gonxha as they boarded the *Marcha* again. "A priest."

The priest was headed for Calcutta, too. Now they had Holy Communion every day. On New Year's Eve they had a sung Mass. *The new year is starting splendidly,* thought Gonxha, *thanks to God*. Once again they anchored, this time in Madras. This was really India. But when they went ashore, Gonxha was stunned.

"The poverty!" she gasped.

Never had she imagined such poverty. Families lived on the streets, lying on mats made of palm leaves. The very poorest had even less. They sprawled on the filthy ground. They were virtually naked. Yet they wore bracelets and rings in their noses and ears. Often their foreheads were marked. One family was gathered around a dead man wrapped in red rags. His face was striped with bright paints. Yellow flowers were arranged on the corpse. None of their efforts to dignify the man's death could soften the horror that chilled Gonxha's heart.

"So this is India," she said to Betike.

Betike couldn't answer.

On January 6, Gonxha and her companions sailed a short way up the Hooghly River to anchor once again. They were in the enormous city of Calcutta, the major city of eastern India. Gonxha felt indescribable joy to at last touch the soil of her province of Bengal. East of the waterfront were throngs of people doing business in bazaars. To the south was an area of lush green parks and elegant Victorian buildings and residences as well as the old Fort William. This side of Calcutta displayed the occupying might of the British. It had been the capital of British India until 1912.

But just as in Madras, there was evidence of squalor everywhere. Human beings seemed to possess nothing but skimpy rags and a few cheap pieces of jewelry. There was no escaping the desperate poverty.

"Calcutta cannot be digested in one visit or two or twenty," said the priest.

"How many people live here?" asked Gonxha.

"Oh, a million, two million." He looked apologetic. "Truthfully, who knows?"

Only God, thought Gonxha. The sisters of Loreto took them to their convent at the Loreto House. In its church they offered thanks to Jesus for a safe trip. They would stay a week at the Loreto House before going on to Darjeeling.

Calcutta was in its very driest, coolest months. January rainfall averaged a mere half inch. Daily temperatures reached 80 degrees Fahrenheit but cooled to 50 degrees at night. It was humid but tolerable.

"It's almost as cool now in Calcutta," said one of the sisters, "as it is in Darjeeling's hottest time."

"How much hotter does Calcutta get?" asked Gonxha innocently.

"One hundred degrees in the summer," answered the sister. "It cools to eighty at night."

One of the other sisters added, "It's the rain that makes one slightly uncomfortable in the summer. It rains several inches every month." She added mischievously, "But when it's not raining, you wouldn't know it."

After one week with the sisters, Gonxha and Betike headed north on a train to the very northern limit of Bengal. It was 450 miles from Calcutta. The young ladies watched out of the crowded train as it sped across the green plains deposited by the Ganges. The many branches of the great river writhed around the plain like brown snakes. They scoured the sands of the plain, often cutting each other off. As a result, some branches of the river grew larger. Some grew smaller. Someone told Gonxha that the Hooghly River had once been the main branch, hence the location of Calcutta. Now the Hooghly was smaller. The main branch was far to the east in the Sunderbans, a treacherous area full of man-eating tigers and crocodiles. As they traveled north, Gonxha watched the Hooghly fade away.

"It is probably kept large and navigable at Calcutta only by dredging," she speculated.

As the train sped north, the ubiquitous rice paddies thinned, and Gonxha saw isolated clumps of tropical forests. About halfway through their journey, they crossed the Ganges River, miles wide before it split downstream into its many tributaries east of Calcutta. Usually Gonxha and Betike saw only rough huts or drab mud-brick buildings. But occasionally they would see an enormous palace built in an Italian style that made them feel they were suddenly looking at a cathedral in Rome. That was the way of India: the very few rich against the multitudes of very poor.

"British India is comprised of more than 560 native states," read Betike from a book. "Each of the native states is ruled by a prince, or *maharajah*, who has absolute power within his own state."

She looked up from the book. "Someone told me that in return for stupendous wealth and power within their own states, the maharajahs pledge to support Great Britain in time of war. And they also allow the British government at New Delhi—the 'Raj'—to control all interstate and international relations."

Temples of all sizes and a few mosques could be seen from the train, as well. Mosques were a familiar sight to Gonxha, whose knowledge of Muslims was considerable. Of all religions, it and Judaism were most similar to Christianity. But most Indians in this part of Bengal were Hindus.

"What do you know of Hindus?" she asked Betike in English, which they faithfully practiced speaking to each other.

"Only that their behavior is far simpler than their beliefs." She went on to explain, "They don't eat meat, especially cows. And they marry within their own caste."

"I read about the caste system," Gonxha replied. "It is very old. There were four castes originally with one group of people excluded completely: the untouchables."

Betike glanced around the railway car cautiously. She said softly in Serbo-Croatian, "The system is insidious. They believe in reincarnation. The catch is that one can be reborn into a higher caste only if one stays strictly within the caste one has been born into in this life. So you see, the system maintains itself."

Gonxha answered in Serbo-Croatian, "I read that the castes have been subdivided and subdivided until now there are thousands of castes."

"How can one understand it?"

"Not us," said Gonxha.

"Nor them," said Betike, with a quick glance at the

Indians riding in the car with them.

Traveling in noisy, crowded third class must have emboldened the natives far beyond their usual silent deference to Europeans. It was not long before they began to ask the two young ladies questions: What are you doing in third class? Where are you from? Where are you going? How much money do you make? What kind of cloth is that you are wearing? How do you dye it? What is that thing on your forehead? Is it starched? Are you the kind of missionary that does not believe in children? Their questions filled Gonxha with wonder, then joy! Suddenly, she was struck by the memory of a verse from the book of John: "Jesus saw Nathanael coming to him, and saith of him, Behold an Israelite indeed, in whom is no guile!"

That was exactly how Gonxha felt about these curious Indians. Behold these Bengalis, in whom there is no guile! So this was what they were really like. *What joy!* she thought. What had she done to deserve such riches?

Their train never lost its view of paddies and a few isolated forests, but Gonxha noticed that the forests changed. As the train moved north, the forests looked more like the forests she had seen in the mountains around Skopje. When at last they approached Darjeeling, the trees were evergreens. Abruptly the train rose up out of the forest onto a ridge that had been cleared.

"There is Darjeeling," said Gonxha excitedly.

When Calcutta had been the capital of India for the British, their summer capital had been Darjeeling, just as their summer capital was now in the mountain air of Simla. At incredible expense, the entire government operation was moved twice a year. Nothing was too good for the viceroy, the British official who headed the Raj. The area around Darjeeling had been cleared of forest, and many fine European-style buildings had been built. But they were dwarfed by something else.

"Look!" said Betike, pointing in the distance.

"The Himalayas!"

Snowcapped mountains loomed in the distance. As Gonxha and Betike got off the train in Darjeeling, they were met by some nuns. The conversation quickly turned to the grandeur above them. Such immensities could scarcely be fathomed. To Gonxha, the Himalayas looked no higher than mountains she had seen in the Alps. But she knew these mountains were higher. One enormous mountain due north, the sisters said, was one of the highest peaks in the world. It was called Kanchenjunga. The highest peak, Mount Everest, could be seen to the northwest some days, too, but actually looked smaller because it was farther away.

"Some Germans will attempt to climb to Kanchenjunga's summit this very year," said one of the sisters. "Pray that they don't die in the effort."

Gonxha and Betike soon plunged into their postulancy. Under their black veil, each young woman now wore a soft black coif with ribbons that tied under the chin. Once again, one mistress trained them in everything. Her name was Sister Baptista Murphy.

At first the postulants concentrated on the routine of religious life. Every day they must expect, even desire, Holy Communion and prayers. Many of these activities were done "in common" with a group of sisters. They learned when "silence" and "fusion" were observed.

Silence did not prevent the courtesy of a simple greeting. But to many of the new postulants, it seemed silence reigned everywhere. They were not to talk to novices or sisters. This might lead to such a person becoming their unofficial spiritual adviser. They were allowed times of fusion, or times when they could talk at length, but only with other postulants. And only in a few places like the kitchen and laundry. But these busy places with their many never-ending chores to be done were full of postulants!

Gonxha soon valued silence. The order wisely followed the counsel of the Lord in the book of Luke: "Pray always." How could one pray if people all about her were idly chattering? When one could not pray, thoughts were at least to rest with God whenever possible.

"Not that talk is unpleasant," Gonxha confided to Betike while ironing a habit in the laundry. "After all, it is a gift from God and a pleasure that costs nothing if used discreetly."

Every day they had to examine their conscience at noon and at night. Each week they had confession. The mistress taught them about the scriptures, theology, prayer, and the rule of their order as well as its history. At dinner one of the sisters read aloud the rule of Loreto or lives of the saints. All conversation was in English. The study of Bengali and Hindi would be added later. Eventually they would also teach local boys and girls. Chores were a blessing to be savored. All the saints loved to labor.

Sister Baptista Murphy told Gonxha and Betike, "You have an important decision looming, one customarily taken when you officially become novices, which for you will be in May. You must decide on names for yourselves."

Neither of these girls needed any further explanation. They understood that usually novices took on the name of a saint whom they admired or looked up to. The most inspiring saint to Gonxha was a Carmelite nun from France who had just been made a saint in 1925. In 1927, the pope had declared that she was a patron saint of missions.

This Carmelite nun had been born Therese Martin, the youngest of five sisters. At fourteen, she had a dramatic conversion on Christmas Eve. She realized that because of His love for her, Christ had become small and weak so that she could become as strong as a giant. She was so driven by her love for Christ that she gained an audience with the pope to ask him to let her become a novice at age fifteen. Her autobiography conveyed to Gonxha her profound, joyous simplicity. Tuberculosis killed the "Little Flower," as she was known, when she was only twenty-four. Her religious name was Therese of the Child Jesus. Because one of the other novices also wanted to take the name Sister Therese, Gonxha requested the Spanish spelling of the name: Teresa.

Betike whispered, "So you've asked for the name of the highly esteemed Teresa of Avila, a doctor of the church?"

"Oh no, I'm the 'little' Teresa," Gonxha tried to explain. She began to realize too late that people would forever assume she had taken her name after Teresa of Avila.

On May 24, 1929, Archbishop Ferdinand Perier was in Darjeeling to preach the sermon before the ceremony in which the postulants officially became novices. His Grace was straight and trim, with a neat beard and mustache. Gonxha knew about the archbishop. Although he had been the bishop of the enormous Calcutta diocese for only five years, the forty-four-year-old Belgian Jesuit had been in India for more than twenty years. He had been instrumental in coaxing the Yugoslavian priests to serve in India. And it was their letters to *Catholic Missions* that had captured Gonxha's heart for India. So it seemed God's hand was in it when that very archbishop welcomed her as a novice. Now Gonxha really was Sister Mary Teresa of the Child Jesus.

"Hello, Sister Mary Magdalene," said the new Sister Mary Teresa to Betike in a time of fusion.

The two now wore the habits of novices. The habit was pulled in at the waist by a cincture. The black veil was replaced by a white veil. Around the shoulders was a very large white collar or bib. And the soft black coif was replaced by a stiff white wimple, a very large head covering that went from the forehead, down the cheeks, and under the chin.

"Oh, Sister Mary Teresa," said Betike. "Wimples pinch the faces of many too small. And sometimes they seem to bleach out a face. But your wimple makes your tan skin and dark eyes and broad forehead look positively angelic."

"You spoil me, Sister Mary Magdalene," replied Sister Mary Teresa. "You seem holy to me now in your habit. Pray to God that someday we merit such appearances."

For two years, Sister Mary Teresa of the Child Jesus studied under her novice mistress, Sister Baptista Murphy. The first year was called the canonical year. Once again the novices studied the Bible. They delved into the constitution of their order. They studied the vows they would be taking. What were the deeper meanings?

From small black books called Breviaries, the novices learned to recite the Divine Office in common. The Divine Office was a library of holy readings: short verses of the Bible, psalms, lessons, tales of martyrs, and hymns. A certain selection was read each day. Reading it was a public prayer.

During the second year of the novitiate, they would refine all this knowledge with the spiritual discernment Saint Ignatius of Loyola advocated. Sister Teresa, as she was now usually called by her sisters, also began to teach children in Darjeeling. But that was not enough. She also helped nurses at small medical stations and at the Bengali hospital. She described her experience at the hospital for the *Catholic Missions* magazine:

> *In the hospital pharmacy hangs a picture of the Redeemer surrounded by a throng of suffering people, on whose faces the torments of their lives have been engraved. Each morning, before I start work, I look at this picture. In it is concentrated everything I feel. I think, "Jesus, it is for you and for these souls!"*
>
> *Then I open the door. The tiny veranda is always full of the sick, the wretched, and the miserable. All eyes are fixed, full of hope, on me. Mothers give me their sick children, their gestures mirroring those in the picture in the pharmacy. My heart beats in happiness: I can continue your work, dear Jesus. I can ease many sorrows. I console them and treat them, repeating the words of the best Friend of souls. Some of them I take to church.*
>
> *Many have come from a distance, walking for as*

much as three hours. What a state they are in! Their
ears and feet are covered in sores. On their backs are
lumps and lesions, among the numerous ulcers. Many
remain at home because they are too debilitated by
tropical fever to come. One is in the terminal stage
of tuberculosis. Some need medicine. It takes a long
time to treat everyone and give the advice that is
needed. You have to explain to them at least three
times how to take a particular medicine, and answer
the same question three times. These poor people have
very little education. . . .

I have finished and I am about to shut the door
when another procession of people arrives.

"What brings you here, good people?"

"Misfortune makes us seek your charity, your love,
and your goodness."

Clearly their needs are very real, because such a
journey is not lightly undertaken in India. I tell them
to bring those children whom their doctor is unable to
help, that I have a wonderful medicine for them. They
promise, and do as they say. . . .

Later, a woman with a broken arm arrives.
Then comes a young man who had been stabbed in the
back by some delinquent in a quarrel. Finally a man
arrives with a bundle from which two dry twigs
protrude. They are the legs of a child. The little boy is
very weak. I realize he is near death. . .the poor child!
Weak, and blind—totally blind. With much pity and

love I take the little one into my arms and fold him
in my apron. The child has found a second mother.
"Who so receives a child, receives me," said the divine
Friend of all little ones. The incident of the child is the
crowning point of my working day.[1]

One thing was very clear. None of the wretched people
who came for help were white Europeans. European men
were the *sahibs*, European women the *memsahibs*. Native
Indians deferred to them in every instance. If a sahib or
memsahib walked into a shop, the shopkeeper abandoned
his native customer immediately. In a crowded street, a
native dared not brush up against a sahib.

In any area of India, no matter how remote, a European was whisked to a hotel or at the very least a "traveler's
bungalow" and offered curried chicken and rice. Not so
with an Indian. And it was unthinkable for an Indian to
dine in English clubs or ride a horse on their polo greens.
Most had no notion of the card game called bridge or the
billiard game called snooker. These things were no more
than words to Gonxha herself. But she as well as the natives
did know that British rule or the Raj did not include the
dark-skinned Indians in any of the "finer" things of life.

Once Gonxha overheard a cynical joke. One Indian
asked another, "Which do you hate more: the Raj or the
moneylender?"

"The Raj," answered the other. "The moneylender at
least hopes I won't die before I pay him back. The Raj

doesn't care whether I die or not."

India seethed with discontent. The Hindu leader Gandhi was organizing peaceful resistance to British rule with what he called *satyagraha* or "force of truth." One event consolidated native resistance. The British had taxed salt, which affected every Indian, no matter how poor. In protest, Gandhi led a march of Indians to the sea where they made their own salt. Of course the British arrested the "troublemaker" Gandhi.

His followers pushed ahead without him. The poetess Sarojini Naidu led twenty-five hundred Indians to Dharasana, north of Bombay, where they intended to occupy the government's huge salt pans. The Indians marched right into a line of police wielding metal-tipped *lathis*. Commanded by British officers, the police cracked the skulls of unresisting marchers by the hundreds.

American reporter Webb Miller witnessed and reported the scene, so ghastly and inhuman that it seemed impossible. Soon the world knew all about it. The heavy-handed British rule of India was becoming more and more unpopular.

"Is such barbarism possible," whispered the sisters at Darjeeling, "even here?"

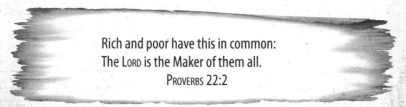

Rich and poor have this in common:
The Lord is the Maker of them all.
Proverbs 22:2

5

THE GREAT COMMISSION

Yes, Darjeeling did seem like a paradise.
Tea estates rolled in gentle terraced hills nearby,
and the Himalayas saw-toothed the distant sky. On May
24, 1931, Sister Mary Teresa of the Child Jesus took her
first vows of poverty, chastity, and obedience.

"By the vow of poverty, I give up my possessions,"
said Sister Teresa, kneeling with the other novices.

Oh God, prayed Sister Teresa, *take these from me.*
Possessions included far more than gold and silver and
trinkets and bank accounts. The sister surrendered her
time and leisure, too.

"By the vow of chastity, I give up my heart's love to
God alone."

Who could doubt the necessity of such a vow? How
could Sister Teresa function without a pure body? And
she was not so naive that she didn't know that chastity

included taking care of her body, her "temple of God," so
it could perform for the Lord at all times.

"By the vow of obedience, I promise to do His will
for me, as shown by my lawful superiors."

Oh yes, prayed Sister Teresa, *let me be obedient.* This
was at the core of all service to the Lord, just below love.

The three vows covered body, mind, and soul. Everything. The vows were to be renewed annually until the
final vows, years away. The professed sisters were now
married to the Lord. They wore a ring on the ring finger
of the right hand. The white veil was replaced by a black
veil. Thus armed for the Lord, Sister Mary Teresa of the
Child Jesus left for Calcutta.

"Good-bye, Darjeeling," she said as she looked back
from the train.

The Himalayas were slightly tainted to her as
she looked back. The Germans were trying to climb

Kanchenjunga again. In her heart, Sister Teresa wished the Germans well, but this time she could not bring herself to say it. The Germans had changed. They had a cancer growing in Germany called the National Socialist Party. It was also called the Nazi Party.

The Nazis stood for everything "progressive." They were not subtle about wanting to rid Germany of everything that wasn't progressive. This included Communists, Jews, dark-skinned people, the mentally disabled, the infirm, and the aged. Of course they had no patience whatever with Sister Teresa's charges: "the sick, the wretched, and the miserable."

When Sister Teresa heard that Germans openly scowled at priests, she prayed, "God help us all. Catholics are soon to join that 'unprogressive' group, too."

The change from the foothills of the mountains to the swamps around Calcutta did not bother Sister Teresa at all. She would now begin her apostolate. Upon arriving in Calcutta, she wove her way through hundreds of indolent bodies lying on the bare floor of the cavernous railway station. Then in a car sent by the sisters, she passed through what seemed an endless maze of narrow streets congested with one-story mud-brick shacks topped by red tile. The rags on the inhabitants advertised their poverty. There was not one tree in sight. Finally, she saw elegant, tall palms, just before the car burst into an open area.

"Loreto Entally!" she exclaimed.

This particular part of eastern Calcutta was called

Entally. And so the compound of the sisters of Loreto was called Loreto Entally. It was enclosed by a wall ten feet high. The wall, painted pale blue, seemed to stretch astonishing distances. The car wedged through a cluster of people selling things by the huge, white-columned gate. On serene green grounds inside the enormous compound were many neat multistoried buildings, some the same blue gray color but some also pale yellow.

The buildings included two high schools for girls run by the superior, Mother Cenacle. The main school had about five hundred boarding students from well-to-do families. They were taught in English. In the other school, about two hundred students were taught in Bengali. These girls ranged from middle class to penniless orphans. As her first duty, Sister Teresa began teaching geography in English. Later she would teach history in English—as well as teaching both subjects in Bengali.

Her history had to include the history of Christianity in India. Sister Teresa was excited to let the girls know that that history went back to the apostles. Tradition said that Saint Thomas had come to India sometime after the resurrection of Christ, then continued on into China, only to return to India where he died.

That story took on new meaning for Sister Teresa now that she had seen some of India herself and heard more details about Saint Thomas. He had settled in Malabar on the southwest coast of India for a while. But he was martyred on the southeast coast and buried at

Mylapore just outside Madras. The very spot south of the Aydras River had been pointed out to Sister Teresa when she had been there. But at the time her heart had been full of doubt, the very sentiment for which the apostle was famous!

"Now I believe," she said once she had spent some time in India. "Why wouldn't he have carried out the Great Commission here in India?"

The evidence was even more compelling that Christians arrived from Syria in the sixth century. At Kerala, Christians retained a Syriac order of service. Then of course there was the irrefutable fact that Saint Francis Xavier, the Jesuit from Portugal, arrived at Goa in 1542. At first the church had concentrated on higher caste Hindus because they were more literate. But eventually the church abhorred discrimination due to the caste system.

Protestants followed suit. Early in the 1600s, both the Dutch and English had established themselves in the Bengal area. The best-known Protestant missionary worked near Calcutta. William Carey had worked tirelessly to translate the Bible, succeeding in many native dialects before his death in 1834. The middle 1800s was a booming period for missions. India soon had twenty Catholic bishops.

"Of course the girls must know of the efforts of our own order," enthused Sister Teresa, as she prepared to teach history to her students.

On August 23, 1841, seven nuns and six postulants sailed from Ireland for India aboard the *Scotia*. It was almost New Year's Day when they disembarked at Calcutta. The head of the diocese, Bishop Carew, had already bought a house for them. The residence at 5 Middleton Row was very large, with many rooms and rich oriental trappings. The sisters quickly rid the house of all extravagance to set up classrooms and simple living quarters for themselves and boarders. This first house was to become known as the Loreto House.

Nearby, next to the chicken market, was an orphanage called Murgi Hatta that was run by the church. By January 10, 1842, the sisters had not only opened the doors of Loreto House to pupils, but had also started classes at the orphanage. The sisters earned such a lofty reputation for exhibiting and building high moral character that Indians were eager to entrust the education of their daughters to them.

"Forty-two sisters died in the first twenty years," Sister Teresa told her students. "And yet they kept coming."

Sister Teresa was in that very tradition. The self-denial and sacrifice that would have crushed an ordinary person only strengthened her. The love of Christ overpowered any hardship. Oh, how she loved her hard but orderly life in Loreto. The nuns rose before dawn. They prayed and read prescribed lessons in the Breviary, Psalms, other Old Testament books, New Testament books, and books by fathers of the church and the saints. Then they attended services, taking communion. Every evening they prayed at vespers and benediction.

And, of course, the sisters taught morning and afternoon, as well as ministering to the needs of their young boarders. The strength to live such a demanding life with joy could come only from sharing in the love of the heavenly Father and His Son.

Once a year each sister was allowed a retreat to deepen her commitment. Sisters were never allowed to leave their enclosure without a pressing reason, and then only with a companion. Yet Sister Teresa saw wrenching poverty outside the compound and began to wonder if she was making such a sacrifice after all.

"As obedient as I am, Lord," she prayed, "my great joy inside the compound begins to feel like a thorn in my side."

A letter from Albania in 1932 informed Sister Teresa that Agatha had joined Lazar in Tirana. Agatha had secured a job translating Serbo-Croatian into Albanian. Mama refused to join them, so now she was alone in Skopje. Agatha wrote that she and Lazar asked Mama again and again to join them in Tirana. News of Mama's isolation disturbed Sister Teresa. She prayed Mama's resistance to leaving Skopje would weaken. But letters from Mama carried no complaint. Mama insisted that she cherished every moment Gonxha was gone because it meant she had kept her faith and her commitment to the church.

The year 1932 also saw the Indian struggle against British rule continue. The Hindu leader Gandhi and thirty-five thousand others of the National Congress were imprisoned. Meanwhile, the British announced they would allow the untouchables to hold separate elections so they could elect representatives to the provincial legislatures. Gandhi protested this, announcing he would starve himself to death in prison.

"His own followers are baffled by him," said one Indian student. "It would seem the British want to advance the cause of the untouchables."

"But Mahatma Gandhi insists the British merely want to institutionalize the caste of untouchables," countered another student.

Gandhi was an original. One could never be sure what the sixty-three-year-old leader would do next. Gandhi might startle onlookers by leading them in his favorite Christian hymn, "Lead Kindly Light." He knew the Sermon on the Mount by heart.

Sister Teresa knew that wherever the emaciated Gandhi went in India, immense crowds gathered. Tens of thousands of people. Most Indians knew little of his politics. All knew he cared for them. Here was one authority who cared if they lived or died.

Sister Teresa had heard with disappointment that Gandhi defended the old caste system. He was himself of the Vaisya caste. Some said he defended the caste system simply because its destruction would undermine the heritage that unified the Indians.

Perhaps his objection to institutionalizing the untouchables came because Gandhi had finally decided the caste system was too unjust to continue. In his usual unpredictable way, he said he didn't care a whit for what he had said twenty years before. He cared only for truth.

He was a powerful moral force—so powerful the Indians called him *Mahatma*, "the soul." If he starved himself to death in prison, the Indians might rebel. And no matter how repressive the British were, they could not withstand a rebellion of several hundred million Indians.

"What turmoil is loose in the world," reflected Sister Teresa. She remembered a saying from Saint Bernard, "Peace within the cell; fierce warfare without."

The ferocity of world events could scarcely be ignored. Germany was more and more openly evil. The leader of the Nazi Party was a diabolical man named Adolf Hitler.

It was no comfort to reflect on what was happening in Italy where the pope resided. Italy had its own version of Hitler: Benito Mussolini. He leaned first one way and then another. But his warped views of society, his disdain for all "nonprogressives" made him a soul mate of Hitler.

In the midst of all this turmoil, Sister Teresa realized she would be a poor servant of Christ if she neglected her own charges. So she labored hard to learn Bengali. After all, she was soon to teach history and geography in the Bengali school.

Bengali would be her fifth language. Already she knew Albanian, Serbo-Croatian, Latin, and English. It was a comfort when she first realized Bengali's symbols were written horizontally from left to right like all European languages. Words were separated by a space, too. Splendid. Bengali was also phonetic, in that each symbol of its alphabet corresponded to a defined sound. But there the similarities ended.

"The symbols for the alphabet are startling in their foreignness," she told her instructor.

"It won't be much harder than the Cyrillic alphabet used by the Greek Orthodox in your homeland," reassured her instructor.

Sister Teresa had never learned that alphabet. "How many vowel symbols are there in Bengali?" she asked uncertainly.

"Eleven."

"And consonants?"

"There are thirty-three. Oh, but there are thirteen vowel-consonant combinations to learn, too."

"Eleven, thirty-three, thirteen," mulled Sister Teresa. "Do the symbols in their alphabet total fifty-seven?"

"More or less."

"If it is God's wish, I will learn Bengali," she said brightly. "Besides, then I will have the alphabet mastered for Hindi."

"I'm sorry," replied her instructor apologetically, "but Hindi has its own alphabet."

By 1935, twenty-five-year-old Sister Teresa was not only very busy with her teaching, but she also helped several nuns with their examinations. She nursed the sick, as well. And the pastor of the Church of Saint Teresa arranged another task for Sister Teresa: to teach at their school for day pupils, the poorest of the poor. Sister Teresa wrote:

> When they saw me for the first time, the children wondered whether I was an evil spirit or a goddess. For them there was no middle way. Anyone who is good is adored like one of their gods; anyone who is ill-disposed is feared as though he were a demon, and kept at arm's length.
>
> I rolled up my sleeves immediately, rearranged the whole room, found water and a broom, and began to sweep the floor. This greatly astonished them. They had never seen a schoolmistress start lessons like that, particularly because in India cleaning is something that the lower castes do; and they stood staring at me for a long time. Seeing me cheerful and smiling, the girls began to help me, and the boys brought

MOTHER TERESA ON LOVING ONE'S NEIGHBOR:

It is not enough for us to say: "I love God," but I also have to love my neighbor. St. John says that you are a liar if you say you love God and you don't love your neighbor. How can you love God whom you do not see, if you do not love your neighbor whom you see, whom you touch, with whom you live?

me more water. After two hours that room was at least in part transformed into a clean schoolroom. It was a long room, which had originally been a chapel and is now divided into five classes.

When I arrived there were fifty-two children, and now there are over three hundred. . . . When I first saw where the children slept and ate, I was full of anguish. It is not possible to find worse poverty. And yet, they are happy. Blessed childhood! Though when we first met, they were not all joyful. They began to leap and sing only when I put my hand on each dirty little head. From that day onwards they call me Ma, which means "Mother." How little it takes to make simple souls happy! The mothers started bringing their children to me to bless. At first I was amazed at this request, but in the missions you have to be prepared for anything.[1]

Sister Teresa spent every minute of every day devoted to the Lord. World events were dismaying to many. But not to one who knew God was the master of history. Why worry? God was in control. And His plan could not be comprehended by humans.

That didn't mean Sister Teresa applauded everything that happened. Of course not! She realized that many things were evil and not of God. When Mussolini invaded Ethiopia in October 1935, it was certainly not something to cheer about. And when he openly sided with Hitler one year later, the news was ominous. But Sister Teresa could not do one thing more than she was doing.

Once in a while during a retreat she had a twinge of regret. Yes, she could not be busier than she was now in Calcutta, but what about the poorest of the poor? Of course she taught such children. But what of the older ones? She walked through the slums to the school at Saint Teresa. The wretched ones were everywhere in the streets. Many dying. She was not reaching them. But what could Sister Teresa do? She must be obedient.

She secured permission to visit the poor on Sundays. Somehow the school at Saint Teresa had freed her a bit from enclosure. She wrote:

Each Sunday I visit the poor in the slums of Calcutta. I cannot be of material assistance to them, for I have nothing; but I go to make them happy. Last time, at least twenty children were anxiously awaiting their

Ma. When they saw me they ran up, all hopping along on one leg. In that building, twelve families live; each family has a single room, two meters long and a meter-and-a-half wide. The doors are so narrow I can scarcely squeeze through them, the ceilings so low it is impossible to stand erect. And these poor people have to pay four rupees for those hovels; if they do not pay promptly, they are thrown out on the street. I am no longer surprised that my pupils love their schools so much, nor that so many are ill with tuberculosis.

One poor woman never complained of her poverty. I was sad, and at the same time happy, to see how my arrival gave her joy. Another said to me, "Oh, Ma! Come again—your smile has brought the sun into our house." On the way home I thought, Oh God, how easy it is to bestow happiness in that place! Give me the strength to be ever the light of their lives, so that I may lead them at last to You![2]

On May 24, 1937, Sister Teresa took her final vows of poverty, chastity, and obedience at Darjeeling. The archbishop of Calcutta, Monsignor Ferdinand Perier, presided at the service. A witness was Father Aloiz Demsar, a Jesuit, who wrote of the event to his superior. His superior in Zagreb, Yugoslavia, was none other than Franjo Jambrekovich, Sister Teresa's spiritual father in Skopje.

Something else awaited her after that. Almost immediately, she succeeded Mother Cenacle as superior of the high school. Not everyone wanted to hear of that development, as she wrote later:

> *A small child came up to me, pale and mournful. He asked whether I would be coming back to them, because he had heard that I was going to become Mother. He began to cry, and through his tears he said, "Oh, don't become Mother!" I held him to me and asked him, "What is the matter? Do not worry. I will be back. I will always be your Ma." The little boy broke into smiles and went back into the courtyard, skipping happily.* [3]

Sister Teresa didn't allow herself to think what she might have done to succeed Mother Cenacle as mother superior of the high school. Surely she was undeserving. Her life seemed overwhelmingly blessed at only twenty-six years old. She had at last taken her final vows. She was in charge of a school. She was no longer Sister Teresa, but Mother Teresa. Moreover, she was also head of the Daughters of Saint Anne, an associated order founded by the sisters of Loreto. These sisters were Indians who taught in Bengali. Each wore the native sari, white in summer and blue in winter.

There was also a sodality for girls in grades six through eleven. The director was Father Julien Henry. He and Father Celeste Van Exem, both Jesuits from Belgium, arrived on the same boat in 1938. Father Henry was slightly older than Father Van Exem, who was himself just slightly older than Mother Teresa.

Father Henry told Mother Teresa, "Your girls in the sodality must not concern themselves only with spirituality inside the Loreto compound."

Surrounding the compound were slums, or *bustees*, Hindu on one side, Muslim on the other. Soon Mother Teresa had the girls venturing forth in groups to visit poor families. They drew water for them and helped in any way they could. They also visited hospitals where they cheered or consoled patients and wrote letters for them. Their efforts were necessarily limited. Mother Teresa could rarely accompany the girls on any of these efforts to help the poor because of the rule of enclosure. As obedient as she was, her limitations still felt like a thorn in her side.

And yet Mother Teresa's own limited work among the poorest of the poor was rich beyond imagination. To think she could make those people so happy. If only she had more time for the poor. A letter from Mama jolted her. Instead of elaborate praise for her new position as mother superior, Mama chided her:

> *Dear child, do not forget that you went out to India*
> *for the sake of the poor. Do you not remember our*
> *File? She was covered in sores, but what made her*
> *suffer much more was the knowledge that she was*
> *alone in the world. We did what we could for her. But*
> *the worst thing was not the sores, it was the fact that*
> *she had been forgotten by her family.*[4]

So Mama, so far away, knew Mother Teresa's dilemma! But of course she did. Who had cleaned and fed more destitute people in Skopje than Mama? Who had instilled love for the poor in little Gonxha? It all came down to the ultimate virtue: love. Love is what the poor needed. And love was proved by helping them. Love begets love.

But Mother Teresa was moving up the ecclesiastical ladder, farther away from the poor who needed her so desperately. Her heart ached, knowing this paradox would haunt her. Some days it was like a storm building inside her.

> He has showed you, O man, what is good. And what does the LORD require of you? To act justly and to love mercy and to walk humbly with your God.
>
> MICAH 6:8

6

CALCUTTA IN TURMOIL

By 1939, the outside world stormed around Mother Teresa. In India, Mahatma Gandhi had come out of retirement at the age of seventy. He fasted in protest over a British agreement with the ruler of the state of Rajkot. When the British acquiesced to Gandhi, it proved the old man still had more influence than any other native leader in India.

But this squabble soon seemed minor compared to world events. By late 1939, Germany began conquering Europe. It was another war involving Britain. Immediately Gandhi and the National Congress demanded Britain state its war aims to Indians. When Britain dragged its feet, the Indian leaders insisted this was one war in which Indians would not participate. But the Muslims in India declared their support for the British war effort.

"Yet one more example of endless war and depravity

looms larger," reflected Mother Teresa.

After all, how could she ignore Europe? She was very
worried about her family. She had seen the war coming
sooner than most. Italy had invaded Albania in April of
1939, though most of the world scarcely noticed. Although an officer in the defeated army, Lazar survived.
He was even able to move his family to Italy because
his wife was Italian. But Agatha and Mama remained in
Albania.

In 1940, a pact among Germany, Italy, and Japan
caused more alarm. Japan, so near India, was very strong
militarily. They had been testing the waters of the Pacific
Ocean for years, always probing for weakness or lack of
will. On December 7, 1941, Japanese dive bombers struck
the American naval fleet at Pearl Harbor.

The sneak attack was a colossal success for Japan.
America's naval power was muted. This would effectively
keep the Americans from helping Asia for a long while.

The Japanese began aggression against their neighbors in earnest. For years they had skirmished with China. Now they struck the Chinese in force. It seemed like a nightmare that they later attacked Burma, too, pushing the British out.

"Burma borders India," mentioned one of the sisters.

On April 6, 1942, the Japanese bombed Madras!

"India is in this war whether Mahatma Gandhi likes it or not," commented some of the sisters.

Mother Teresa and her sisters of Loreto and Daughters of Saint Anne were in the war, too. The compound at Entally was requisitioned for the war. It became a hospital for the British military. The dormitories became choked with wounded soldiers. Many of the students were sent to cities inland. Some were still taught in Calcutta. Mother Teresa now worked out of a building on Convent Road. Could the war get any worse?

They soon found out. Indians began starving.

"What is the problem?" asked the sisters. "Where is the rice?"

The immense paddy lands of the Bengal had not failed them in recent memory. Hundreds, thousands of fields were scattered along great winding rivers. The rice was delivered to the thronging cities in thousands of boats. The paddy lands were a world apart with their short, isolated dirt roads and white geese and lowing cattle and Brahmins. But now many people flocked into Calcutta, carrying everything they owned in one basket or a box. Where was the rice? Everyone wanted to know.

Soon they found out. All boats had been requisitioned for the war effort. But what of the people? Mother Teresa had learned long ago what the people suspected of the British government, the Raj. The Raj didn't care if they lived or died.

The catastrophe of 1943 seemed to prove it. People were starving everywhere in Bengal. Mothers' milk dried up. Babies died. The numbers of dead staggered the imagination. Ten thousand. One hundred thousand. Finally, one million. Two million! And who but God knew how many more? Every day smoke filled the air as the dead were burned in pyres along the Hooghly River in the Hindu tradition. Gandhi was in prison, silenced. Who could speak for the Indians?

On December 5, 1943, great explosions shattered the wintry coolness in Calcutta.

"Planes are bombing the harbor!" screamed one student who had just rushed into the compound.

"How can it get any worse in Calcutta?" lamented another student.

Yet, after that bomb raid, life began to improve for Calcutta. India had a new viceroy, a new ruler. He was more sensitive to the needs of the Indians. Although the war in Asia had never looked grimmer for the British, boats began to deliver rice again. Thus ended one of the greatest famines in the history of the world, seemingly lost in the greatest war in the history of the world. Would several million dead Bengalis even get a footnote in history books? Mother Teresa taught history. Somehow she doubted it.

But she knew God's will for her. "I can no more protest the evil leaders of the Raj than Saint Paul protested the evil leaders of the Roman Empire."

But Indians did protest. Some even joined the Japanese armies in Burma. Their battle cry was "Asia for Asians!"

Japan sensed 1944 was the right moment for conquering India. In March they bombed airfields in the Naga Hills which bordered Burma six hundred miles northeast of Calcutta. That same month they surged across the Chindwin River. British and Indian forces fought them between the Chindwin and the largest city in the Naga Hills, Imphal. By the end of the month, Imphal was cut off, and three Indian divisions were trapped—including perhaps forty thousand men.

"Pray for the monsoons to come early," said Mother Teresa, "because it seems nothing else will stop the fighting and killing."

But April was one month too early for the drenching monsoon rains. Soon, Kohima, a second major city, was surrounded by the Japanese. Still, the besieged Indian troops held out. On April 15, a rumor swept India like early monsoon winds. The British military head-quarters were being moved from New Delhi. In fact, they were being moved from India! They were being moved all the way south to Ceylon.

Then came stunning news.

Indian forces counterattacked in force. For weeks British and Indian troops had secretly gathered in the area next to the Japanese invaders. Now as the monsoons struck, so did they. The Japanese reeled back in confusion. By the end of June, they were out of India, leaving behind thirty thousand dead soldiers.

By the middle of 1944, Gandhi was out of prison. It seemed that now the war was really over for India. The situation that had looked so hopeless for Britain and its allies early in 1944 had completely reversed. The Japanese were being pummeled in Burma and out in the Pacific.

Even the lunatic Hitler was being clobbered. The allies had invaded Europe in June. Raging east across Europe were the most powerful armies in the history of the world. The Russians were advancing against Hitler from the east. The vile Nazi empire was about to fall.

"And the Raj in India looks like it may fall at last, too," said some of Mother Teresa's students.

Could it be? In September of 1944, newspapers carried reports of correspondence between Gandhi and M. A. Jinnah, the leader of the Muslims. The two men virtually negotiated the nature of the independent state or states that would result from British withdrawal. Were the British willing? Perhaps at long last they were!

But independence was not simple. Gandhi wanted a united India. After all, 90 percent of Muslims were converted Hindus. They shared common languages and customs. Hindu or Muslim, they were Indian through and through. But Jinnah insisted on some kind of autonomy for Muslims. Perhaps they could finally agree on some subregions of India under Muslim control.

The year 1945 brought startling changes. By summer the Germans and Japanese were defeated. In Italy, Lazar made more money than he had ever made in his life by simply driving the jeep of an officer in the occupying American forces. In July the British voted out their prime minister and great war leader, Winston Churchill. This was highly significant for India because Churchill had been the most vociferous opponent to Indian independence. His successor as prime minister of Britain, Clement Attlee, wanted independence for India and said so in September.

"The way seems clear," said Mother Teresa's students in wonder.

In December both Gandhi and the new viceroy, Archibald Wavell, were in Calcutta. "Avoid strife," Wavell urged thousands of Indians. "You are at the gate of political and economic opportunity."[1] The seventy-six-year-old

Mahatma echoed his message, imploring peace, before being taken to an *ashram*, or refuge, eight miles from the city. Indians fell to revere the very dust his car had driven over.

Mother Teresa pondered the warnings of both Wavell and Gandhi. Great danger must lie ahead. And in fact, month after month the Hindu leaders and Muslim leaders bickered. Speculation was endless. Some people hoarded food. Some began to starve. Riots broke out. Muslims killed Hindus. Hindus killed Muslims. The British announced they would be leaving India in 1948, whether the Indians ever agreed among themselves or not! Surely that would stop the strife.

"Still the Hindu and Muslim leaders bicker," grumbled some of the students.

On August 16, 1946, the sisters inside the Loreto compound found out just how terrible it had become in Calcutta. Men—Hindus and Muslims alike—began scaling the ten-foot walls of the Loreto compound to hide. The Loreto compound was located between two neighborhoods. The Muslims lived in Moti Jihl, the neighborhood on one side of the compound. On the other side were the potteries and tanneries of Tengra, where Hindus lived. The men inside the Loreto compound were fleeing because they had been caught in the wrong neighborhood at the wrong time.

It seemed that Muslims had gathered that day for a rally in the great green park of Calcutta called the Maiden.

Hindus agitated them. Fights broke out. The fighting spread like wildfire. Hindus and Muslims were killing each other. Blood flowed over the streets of Calcutta. There was scant gunfire. Indians used lathis and knives and hatchets. Killing was silent, except for the screams of the victims. The sisters led the Muslims through their peaceful compound to Moti Jihl. Hindus were led through the compound to the Tengra neighborhood.

Soon afterward, a sister in charge of the commissary confronted Mother Teresa. "We will not escape this calamity, Mother. Calcutta is not functioning. We are almost out of food."

Three hundred girls were in their care. What could be done? Mother Teresa knew only too well what she had to do. She prayed for God's help first. Then she alone went outside the compound walls, walking the bloody streets of Calcutta. Bodies, slashed and severed and bled dry, defiled the street. No wonder the poor men had fled into the compound!

"What are you doing there?" screamed someone.

It was a truck. Soldiers!

"I have three hundred girls in the Loreto compound," explained Mother Teresa. "We have no food. Soon we will be starving."

"Well, you can't walk the streets!"

Miraculously the soldiers found bags of rice and delivered them and Mother Teresa to the compound. Once again, God had provided.

Meanwhile Calcutta was in the grip of insanity. The mayhem became more violent. A few became murderers inspired by the devil. They would venture into neighborhoods with homemade kerosene bombs and set houses ablaze. If their imagined enemies were caught inside, so much the better, cackled the murderers. The killing lasted four endless days. The first day was already referred to as the Day of the Great Killing.

"Five thousand dead," said one of Mother Teresa's stunned students.

"We're not all murderers," blurted one distressed student. "Several people were killed trying to defend their friends of the opposite faith."

On September 10, 1946, less than one month after the Day of the Great Killing, Mother Teresa went to Sealdah Station and boarded a train to Darjeeling for her annual retreat. Some might have questioned Mother Teresa taking her retreat at that time. How could she go to Darjeeling when such terrible things had just happened in Calcutta? But they did not understand Saint Ignatius of Loyola and obedience.

Mother Teresa hardly needed to look out the window as the train rumbled north across the flat plains scoured by the Ganges. She had made this trip many times before. Everywhere glimmered the wetlands of the rice paddies. Suddenly, the roar of the train was overwhelmed by a voice!

Go to the poor. Leave the convent. Live with the poorest of the poor.

Mother Teresa did not doubt the source for one moment. It was God's voice. He was commanding her to leave the convent and live with the poor! But leave the convent? How? She had taken vows of enclosure. Live with the poor? How? There was no procedure for this. There was no novitiate for this. There was no mother superior to guide her. There was no convent to shelter her.

"Yet it is obvious God has told me on the way to my retreat," she reflected, "because He intends for me to meditate and pray on it."

And that's exactly what she did. At thirty-six, she had searched her heart on these retreats for seventeen years, guided by Saint Ignatius of Loyola's *Spiritual Exercises*. In the first stage she once again reinforced her conviction of sin and God's forgiveness. Then she dwelt for a long time on the fact that Christ is active in the world. Then came the question: How best could she help Him? Every minute of every hour of every day strengthened her conviction that she must leave the convent and live with the poorest of the poor. That was God's will for her. Helping every poor person she could help would be like helping Christ Himself. It was her calling within a calling.

"But how can I, a cloistered nun, accomplish it?" she prayed. "I can't, O Lord, but You can."

She returned to Calcutta in October.

At the Loreto compound, Mother Teresa shared her conviction on this new calling with her spiritual adviser, Celeste Van Exem, the Jesuit priest who also pastored a church at Baithak Khana. Father Van Exem couldn't hide his astonishment. This tiny woman, he seemed to be thinking, venturing out into the bloody streets of Calcutta? Hadn't she better pray on it some more? Mother Teresa handed him a sheaf of papers describing her call and everything she had discerned spiritually during the retreat. She would dress in a sari as an Indian and live in the poorest slums!

"You have the right to petition the Congregation for the Propagation of the Faith in Rome," he told her numbly, "and ask to be released from your vows."

"Is there another way?" she prodded cautiously.

"Advise your archbishop here. Let him be your guide."

So when Archbishop Ferdinand Perier visited the Loreto compound in late 1946, Mother Teresa approached him for an audience. She told him everything. He listened patiently. He didn't seem startled by such an unorthodox request. Perhaps it had happened before. Perhaps he had already been briefed.

Although his face was sober, unreadable, it was as if she could read his mind. This nun was virtually asking to leave her order and start a new one. He couldn't himself approve such a huge step. Rome would have to decide. Of course, he could advise her in the strongest terms to drop the whole thing. After all, her calling seemed in the realm of impossibilities. It was a murderous time in Calcutta, the worst in anyone's memory.

But the archbishop didn't discourage her. Why should he doubt that Mother Teresa thought she had heard this calling from God just as she said? And who could know if this calling she heard was not the direct word from God just as she said? With God anything is possible. The archbishop could have demanded a sign for himself that this was God's will for her. But he didn't.

"Bless you, Sister, for telling me," he said, concluding the audience.

Soon Mother Teresa found she was being sent 130 miles away to Asanol for medical attention! Was this the archbishop's answer? Did he believe only a very sick woman could hallucinate such a vision? The doctors at Asanol examined her for a lung infection. Was she coming down with tuberculosis? As far back as her youth in Skopje she had coughed more than normal and Mama had worried about her lungs. Was the condition at long last serious?

"No," the medical people admitted.

She returned to her school, cautioned to rest instead of driving herself constantly. But at the school, students caught up in the events sweeping India were squabbling among themselves. She found two factions pitted against each other: Hindu against Muslim. No one could pacify them. Was this why Mother Teresa was called back so soon? Was this a test for her? No matter. Her duty was clear. Mother Teresa called the leaders of the two factions together. Within half an hour the situation was calm, the girls repentant.

"Mother is back," whispered one girl to another. "Everything is all right again."

And what of her calling within a calling? Mother Teresa suspected the archbishop was probing every possibility. Although he had been in India for forty years, he scarcely knew the poorest of the poor. To his credit, he socialized with Indians as well as Europeans at the very democratic Calcutta Club. But these wealthy Indians probably knew the poorest of the poor no better than the Europeans did. Mother Teresa in no way judged him though. For the good of the church, an archbishop had to deal with matters too political, too financial, too diplomatic for a simple teaching nun to know about.

"Is such a wild thing practical?" he was probably asking knowledgeable people. Could a tiny European woman dressed as a native go into the slums at this time in India's history? Would she be safe from attack from zealots? Even if she was safe, would she be accepted? Could she recruit Bengali girls as sisters as she wished?

Then Mother Teresa heard that years before a nun had requested almost exactly what she had requested: a mission among the poor outside the enclosure. The archbishop had asked her to contemplate on her request for one year. After one year the nun had changed her mind!

"Is that it?" she wondered. "Is the archbishop waiting

for me to change my mind?"

Soon however, the archbishop got in touch with Mother Teresa. "Why don't you try it with the Daughters of Anne? They are Bengali women. And you already work with them."

So he approved! He had been probing problems and possibilities. The answers he sought must have been encouraging. It was becoming more obvious, though, that the archbishop did not want to approach Rome. The Vatican was very resistant to new orders. There were so many already.

Mother Teresa must not speculate about the future but obey her present instructions. She approached the Daughters of Anne. She soon found them very difficult. They already had their own traditions, their own ways of doing things. As mother superior she had no desire to debate everything she wanted to do because it differed from the rigid way they had done it before. With much regret she saw the archbishop.

"My plan cannot work with the Daughters of Anne," she told him.

The archbishop must have groaned inside. Not only were the Daughters of Anne now worried about their future because there might be a new order in Calcutta similar to their own, but the obvious needs of an entirely new order were overwhelming.

"It won't happen overnight," he told Mother Teresa grimly. He would have to ask Rome for permission to start a new religious order. In the meantime Mother Teresa would need permission from the mother general of her order to go outside the convent. After all, she had taken vows not to.

"Not to mention the fighting that still flares up in Calcutta," added the worried archbishop. "There has been no real peace since the Day of the Great Killing. Gangs roam about now, looking for trouble. Just recently, thirty-two died in one day."

It seemed all the archbishop could do to keep from throwing up his arms in dismay. But support her he did. And Mother Teresa did what she had to do and left the success or failure of her second calling in God's hands. She thought about the rule or constitution her new order would need. She even thought about her very first efforts outside the convent. They could not be small. The archbishop had already told her that once outside, she must recruit ten novices.

All of 1947 passed. Mother Teresa waited. India did not. In August two countries were created: India for the Hindus and Pakistan for the Muslims. But political problems were not over. Hindus began to force Muslims left in Hindu India to convert to their faith. Muslims began to force Hindus left in Muslim Pakistan to convert to their faith. Resentment festered. Hindus began to slaughter the Muslims left in Hindu India. Muslims began to slaughter the Hindus left in Muslim Pakistan. Millions of refugees were flooding to safety. Atrocities were committed that staggered the imagination. Babies were ripped apart. Women were stuffed down wells.

"Will the madness ever end?" wondered the sisters.

In Calcutta, it seemed riots had been going on forever. Gandhi was in the city, trying to set an example by living with a Muslim friend. Hooligans burst into the house, threatening to kill Gandhi himself. Gandhi was saved, but he was so disgusted he announced September 1 that he would fast unto death if the violence did not end. At the age of seventy-eight and weighing barely one hundred pounds, he wouldn't last long.

His demands were severe. Leaders of the hooligan gangs all over Calcutta must come to him personally and sign a pledge that they would not fight again. Miraculously they did, many in tears.

"Gandhi has stopped the fighting in Calcutta!" rejoiced the students.

The rest of India was not so fortunate. Fighting still flared up again and again all over. Gandhi shuffled about, trying to put out every fire. How long could this frail old man last? Then in January 1948, in New Delhi, the unthinkable happened.

> There will always be poor people in the land. Therefore I command you to be open-handed toward your brothers and toward the poor and needy in your land.
>
> DEUTERONOMY 15:11

7

MISSIONARIES OF CHARITY

January 1948. Gandhi was murdered. By a Hindu who didn't want Gandhi to make peace. And the fighting continued. Mother Teresa fought despair. Would anything good ever come out of these ashes? Then in August of that year, she got news of her own fate.

"Praise God for His mercy," she said.

At long last, permission to proceed had been granted! Mother Teresa could venture out of the convent and begin a new diocesan order. She had decided to call her order Missionaries of Charity. What else did she have to give but love? It was up to the archbishop's discretion how much time he granted for her to make this new order a success. He granted her one year.

Much of her work would be ministering to the sick, so Mother Teresa immediately wrote the Medical Mission Sisters in Patna. Could she stay there, she asked, and get medical training? She had done such work as a novice, but she needed a refresher. The Medical Mission Sisters quickly gave her permission, and days later she arrived at their convent in a section of Patna called Padri ki Haveli.

She knew they were taken aback by her appearance. This was no Loreto mother superior in long black habit and stiff white coif. She wore an ankle-length white cotton frock with a band collar and long sleeves under the wrapping of a sari like the native women wore!

"The new diocesan order of the Missionaries of Charity wear this habit," she explained.

Every day she was at Holy Family Hospital. Every time a patient entered, Mother Teresa rushed to observe. She saw cholera and smallpox. She saw tuberculosis. She saw the dreaded leprosy. Soon she was doing more than observing. She ministered to the patients. She held their hands, many of them while dying, to console them.

She was no longer in Bengal where natives spoke Bengali. She had to speak Hindi, which she had learned at the convent after she learned Bengali.

When not with a patient, she was taught the basics of changing beds, washing patients, and giving injections. She even assisted in the delivery of babies!

At dinner she told the sisters, "Missionaries of Charity nuns will eat the humblest of Bengali diets: rice and salt."

"Oh no!" objected one of the sisters who was a doctor. "That would be a sin! You would doom your girls to death from tuberculosis and other diseases. You must cure the sick, not join them!"

"Yes," objected another. "Don't forget your vow to keep the body pure."

It sounded like a lecture. But Mother Teresa didn't mind. Apparently a diet of only rice and salt was a bad idea. Not that she had any sisters yet. Or even a ministry.

She ran many of her ideas past the outspoken sisters at Patna. They approved very much of her cotton sari for a habit. But it would have to be washed daily if working with the sick. Did she have a laundry yet? "I have no laundry yet," replied Mother Teresa.

She must keep her sisters strong with a balanced diet and rest during the long, exhausting work day. What are your kitchen and dormitories like? "I have nothing yet," replied Mother Teresa.

You must give your girls one day off a week, continued the sisters, unperturbed by the impossibility of Mother Teresa's plans. Your girls must have their retreat to look forward to once a year, they insisted. And the Medical Mission Sisters all thought one could not mix ministering to the poor and ministering to others. Mother Teresa must confine her efforts only to the poor.

After so much discussion, it was hard to remember which ideas had been hers originally and which ones the sisters planted there. But what did it matter? Weren't they God's answers to her prayers anyway?

"What will you do first?" they asked her.

"I don't know," replied Mother Teresa.

"Let these carry you on your mission," they said, and gave her a brand-new pair of very sturdy sandals.

After she returned to Calcutta, the momentous day came: December 8, 1948. She stepped out onto the cruel streets of Calcutta. She had lived in India nearly twenty years. How she hated leaving her teaching. How she hated leaving the pleasant gardens inside the convent. She really felt while teaching she was the happiest nun on earth.

For two weeks she stayed with the Little Sisters of the Poor at Saint Joseph's Home for the Aged. She learned to work with the aged, as well as venturing forth every day into different slums. What looks of astonishment she drew. What gaping jaws. A European woman dressed in a simple cotton sari? And only sandals on her feet? And no stockings!

After two weeks she had decided where to start. She would start her calling in the Muslim slum of Moti Jihl. She had a few rupees to rent a room in a decrepit shanty.

"In a week or two I will have no money whatever," she admitted to herself. "But God will provide."

The beginning of her calling was almost too small to imagine. Most of the poor watched her suspiciously. A few were unfriendly. Some called her names. Some even threw stones at her. The real hooligans, the *goondas*, had not discovered her yet.

On December 21, 1948, Mother Teresa rounded up

five puzzled children from nearby hovels and sat them in an open space beside Pearl Lake, or Moti Jihl, the scummy pond that gave the bustee its name. She began scratching letters of the Bengali alphabet in the dirt with a stick. And she gave the children the most important thing they could ever get: love. Soon the children looked forward to seeing her every day.

One of the first things they learned was how to keep themselves clean. Mother Teresa herself washed each one the first time. They would be much more resistant to disease now. Besides teaching them hygiene and the alphabet, she taught them manners and religion.

Amazingly, a few people started helping her. She received an *anna*, the smallest coin there was. Another. Then a rupee here. Another rupee. One man brought a table. Then someone brought her a chair. Some offered her food. She begged a merchant for little bars of soap. "Why not?" he shrugged. Her most diligent students were then rewarded with soap. She begged money for food. Soon every child got milk at lunch.

It was not long before she had thirty-five children in her class. She continued to beg. A parish priest in the Park Circus area gave her one hundred rupees. Unbelievably, she began to open a second school, this one in Tiljala, another bustee. Within a month, more than twenty children were showing up there every morning. Most ran, they were so anxious to learn from Ma, a name she continued to be known by.

"Kaw! Khaw! Gaw!" screamed tiny enthusiastic voices, practicing the ABCs of the Bengali alphabet.

Other children were drawn irresistibly to the chorus of learning. So, too, were adult volunteers, laypeople, and even teachers from Saint Mary's who were allowed to leave the Loreto compound to assist her. The number of children at Moti Jihl swelled to forty, fifty, sixty. The number at Tiljala increased, too.

Each day it seemed the children showed up neater and cleaner. Cursing and foul language waned, then stopped. Their obedience to her astonished her. They seemed in a religious order themselves. How desperately they wanted order. How desperately they wanted to learn! Never was Mother Teresa so sure of her second calling. Other subjects were added. Sewing was eagerly learned by the girls. Oh, if they could mend their own clothes, they chirped, or even make them someday!

One helper asked Mother Teresa, "Why not apply for a grant from the Corporation of Calcutta? Perhaps they will subsidize the schools."

"That is tempting."

The corporation was part of the city government. Mother Teresa toyed with the idea. She even went to speak to the inspectress of schools, who was very interested. *Why not?* thought Mother Teresa. Begging was hard. One priest, God forgive him, had treated her rudely when she asked him for money. His eyes carried that deep disgust reserved for beggars. His voice carried revulsion. His hands knotted into resistant fists.

She could not walk down that street where he had repulsed her without feeling the bitter sting. Was she not flesh and blood? Did she not have feelings? She only begged because she remembered the precious Lord himself saying, "I thirst." Some days it was very hard to beg.

But could she become an instrument of the government by asking for its aid? And was she now to convert her children into wards of the government? Would she now have inspectors coming by to tell her what to do and what to say? What could she be thinking of?

"Neither be ye of doubtful mind," she said, remembering the Lord's words in Luke. She decided not to apply for government aid.

Working with such young children was pure joy for Mother Teresa. She taught them a small hymn in Bengali to sing for Father Nicaise, who came by one day to bless the humble outdoor school. The zealous tikes mangled the hymn, yet Mother Teresa could not have been prouder.

And they, little urchins as poor as they were, knew

sympathy. One child whispered to Mother Teresa one day that two of the children, a brother and a sister, had not eaten since the previous morning. The two children were too ashamed to tell her. Class stopped then and there while Mother Teresa rushed off to find food for the two children.

Just as her children astonished her, she seemed to astonish everyone who watched her activities. Occasionally she stopped at the parish school at the Church of Saint Teresa to eat her lunch with Loreto sisters who taught there.

"You want to open a dispensary?" asked pencil-thin Sister Rozario in amazement one day in January. "You've only been out of the Loreto Convent a few weeks!"

"Yes, it's high time then," said Mother Teresa, who knew her one-year trial had actually started in August. "All I need is the space."

Sister Rozario brightened. "What about using a classroom here after school hours?"

Incredibly Mother Teresa soon had a dispensary for the poorest of the poor. All services were free. Long lines waited for her when she arrived in the late afternoon. The main aim of the clinic was to screen for tuberculosis. But they also dispensed pills in cheap tobacco tins. Medicines were stored in wooden crates labeled Headaches, Stomachaches, Diarrhea, and other obvious ailments. Sister Rozario, a sister just eleven years from the Irish convent itself, was thrilled to help Mother Teresa.

MOTHER TERESA ON ENCOURAGEMENT:

If we are contemplatives in the heart of the world with all its problems, these problems can never discourage us. We must always remember what God tells us in scripture: "Even if a mother could forget the child in her womb"—something impossible, but even if she could forget—"I will never forget you."

But Mother Teresa could not depend much longer on the fathers and the sisters, who had their own duties. And perhaps their efforts were more out of pity for her than a conviction for her calling. She no longer liked to visit Entally, because the mother superior always pleaded with her to return to teach. One pastor told Mother Teresa outright she was wasting her time. Whispers reached her. She wrote her anguish in a small journal that the archbishop himself had asked her to keep:

> *I believe some are saying what [is the] use of working among this lowest of the low. . .[because if] the great, the learned and the rich are ready to come, it is better to give full force to them. Yes, let them all do it. If the rich people can have the full service and devotion of so many nuns and priests, surely the poorest of the poor and the lowest of the low can have the love and*

devotion of us few—"the Slum Sister" they call me, and
I am glad to be just that for His love and glory.[1]

But she must have help. Where were her religious
children? Half of her year outside the convent was already gone! Still, she could not add novices to help her
while living in a hovel. She must find someplace suitable.
But she had so little money. In February 1949, she wrote:

> *I am afraid. . .our Lord just wants me to be a*
> *"Free Nun," covered with the poverty of the Cross.*
> *But today I learned a good lesson—the poverty of the*
> *poor must be often so hard for them. When I went*
> *around looking for a home, I walked and walked till*
> *my legs and arms ached. I thought how they must also*
> *ache in body and soul looking for home, food, help.*
> *Then the temptation grew strong. The palace build-*
> *ings of Loreto came rushing into my mind. All the*
> *beautiful things and comforts—in a word everything.*
> *"You have only to say the word and all that will*
> *be yours again," the tempter kept on saying. Of free*
> *choice, My God, and out of love for You, I desire to*
> *remain and do whatever be Your Holy Will in my*
> *regard. I do not let a single tear come, even if I suffer*
> *more than now. I still want to do Your Holy Will.*
> *This is the dark night of the birth of the Society. My*
> *God, give me courage now, this moment, to persevere*
> *in following Your Will.*[2]

Days after Mother Teresa wrote that plea in her journal, which was yet unseen by anyone but herself, her spiritual adviser, Father Van Exem, told her, "I've arranged for you to take a room in a large house owned by the Gomes brothers on Creek Lane."

"That seems like too nice a neighborhood. I can't afford much."

"It's free."

The three-story house was in an old, congested part of Calcutta with the narrowest of streets. Still, the property was not in a slum but had pillared gates and lush trees and shrubs. The house had verandas and an ornate railing on the roof. The Gomes family was Indian, but it was also Roman Catholic, very active in the church. Of the four brothers, two had left to live in Pakistan, encouraged to do so by the archbishop himself. He reasoned such devout Catholics could bolster other Catholics in that sea of Muslims.

Because the two brothers were gone, the entire third floor of the home was vacant. Mother Teresa came to live with the Gomes family in one third-floor room.

Mabel, eight-year-old daughter of Michael Gomes, looked at Mother Teresa very approvingly. It seemed the whole thing was the little girl's idea. Father Van Exem had come to give the last rites to her grandmother. While there the priest inquired if the family knew of some tiny room in the area near Moti Jihl that Mother Teresa could rent for very little. "The upper floor here is empty!" little Mabel had shouted.

So now Mother Teresa lived in a pleasant home rent-free. "'I thank thee, O Father, Lord of heaven and earth, because thou hast hid these things from the wise and prudent, and hast revealed them unto babes,'" quoted Mother Teresa, never having doubted for a moment the profound truth in the Lord's words.

Living with Mother Teresa was her friend Charur Ma, a widow who had been a cook at the convent. Their furniture was nothing more than wooden packing crates. Michael Gomes offered them real furnishings that his brothers had stored, but Mother Teresa refused.

Even with Charur Ma as her companion, at times Mother Teresa suffered from loneliness. And anxiety. How could she found an order without novices? The archbishop wouldn't wait forever for her to attract ten novices.

"So far I have none!" she warned herself.

She couldn't hide her candle under a basket any longer. Using a packing crate as a desk, she worked late into the night writing pleas to former students. But she cautioned them to think long and very hard about such a severe life of sacrifice.

Mother Teresa wrote to one student whom she had taught since grade seven. Subashini Das had been particularly enthusiastic about working with the poor in the sodality. Once Subashini had even pleaded with Mother Teresa to lead them into the slums—and this happened while Mother Teresa's request to leave the Loreto compound was a secret! Surely Subashini Das might be interested.

So Mother Teresa wrote former students and waited. And waited. *Oh Lord, where are my novices?* On a particularly bleak night she recorded:

> *Today, my God, what tortures of loneliness.*
> *I wonder how long my heart will suffer this. Tears*
> *rolled and rolled. Everyone sees my weakness. My*
> *God, give me courage now to fight self and the*
> *tempter. Let me not draw back from the sacrifice*
> *I have made of my free choice and conviction.*[3]

Mother Teresa may have anguished at night, but she toiled unceasingly during the day. One day she took little Mabel with her to Moti Jihl. Usually she had the little girl back home by late afternoon. But this day they came upon a small tragedy. It had rained hard, an unexpected event during the dry season. A poor woman was standing in water up to her knees in a house that was surrounded by a low circular wall but had no roof to speak of. She held a child and was trying to shield it from the rain with an old enamel bowl. Mother Teresa took the child. The child was hot with fever.

"Naturally we had to take the poor dears to the home of a good family I know where they could stay dry for a while," explained Mother Teresa to Mabel's worried parents when they finally returned. "And of course I had to give the poor child some medicine."

A few days later in March, on the Feast of Saint Joseph, Mother Teresa had a visitor in the evening. Her visitor was as bright-eyed and tiny as Mother Teresa herself.

"Subashini Das!" cried Mother Teresa.

"I want to join you," said Subashini.

"Welcome."

Her first novice! She took Subashini to Baithak Khana, the church pastored by Father Van Exem, for her consecration. She became known as Sister Agnes. Days later, a second novice appeared. She was also a former student. She took the name Sister Gertrude. She was tall and sturdy, yet so shy and intimidated by Mother Teresa that for a while she refused to sit on the same bench with her to eat.

Mother Teresa's two novices confessed they loved her very much. During the war, when many of the Loreto sisters evacuated, Mother Teresa had taught more than geography and history. She had taught religion to Subashini so powerfully that the young Bengali couldn't wait to serve Christ. And now what great fortune, cried Subashini, to join her mentor. Timid Sister Gertrude recalled all the special help Mother Teresa had given her. Mother Teresa had huddled her off to the hospital when she was sick. She had tutored her in mathematics.

"I wondered, how can Mother do so much?" marveled

Sister Gertrude. "How can Mother ever sleep? I was just one of hundreds of students!"

The two novices were so energetic, Mother Teresa felt like she was following them. How her little order could serve Jesus now!

School in the open was rained out more each day. They were nearing the monsoon season when having school outside was impossible. The school effort was going far too well to be stopped by bad weather. What could she do?

Mother Teresa begged enough money to rent a large room for the children near the pond in Moti Jhil. In Tiljala, too, she rented a room. Soon they added second rooms. The joy in the tiny birdlike voices, chanting the Bengali alphabet, continued to draw other children like a magnet. The only limits to the number of students they might eventually have were having enough sisters to teach and enough money to buy space and supplies. Mother Teresa was convinced that God would provide. The slum people, poor as they were, wanted desperately for their children to have a better chance in life.

"I must visit the corporation soon," said Mother Teresa to herself. "These people need good germ-free water, not water that stagnates in this pond." And she could visualize a shiny new pump just as easily as she saw neat school buildings popping up here and there.

With sisters helping her, Mother Teresa could attend to other things, such as begging medical supplies or food or whatever else they needed. Before Sister Gertrude came, Mother Teresa always had to accompany Sister Agnes. Now that she had two novices, she could send them out together.

"Be a cheerful giver," she urged them repeatedly. On days when they didn't feel cheerful, she said, they must act cheerfully. They must not minister to poor wretches already depressed and miserable when their own faces were glum and their eyes watery with pity.

"Let the Lord's love take over and shine through!" she taught her novices.

The three women dressed alike. Someday Mother Teresa wanted all of her order to wear heavy white cotton saris bordered with blue stripes. But that would be for professed sisters. For now the cloth was plain white cotton. The women wore it like the traditional Indian sari over an ankle-length habit with long sleeves. The end of the huge cloth was pinned on the left shoulder, and from that pin dangled a tiny cross. They wore sandals with no stockings. Mother Teresa was very satisfied with the no-nonsense way she and her girls looked.

"But where are the other eight sisters I need, Lord?" she prayed.

Mother Teresa knew that the clock was running out.

A generous man will himself be blessed,
for he shares his food with the poor.
PROVERBS 22:9

8

"I THIRST"

A third girl joined her order. Then a fourth. Like the others, Sisters Dorothy and Margaret Mary had to quickly develop a powerful faith that somehow God would provide. For Mother Teresa was not like those worldly people who prospered in the outside world. The worldly had learned to ignore the begging palms of the poorest of the poor. Mother Teresa, without hesitating, would give the poor every last rupee she had. All they had to do was ask. Many a time, the sisters had to suffer long walks because Mother Teresa had given away their streetcar money, or they had to eat less at dinner because Mother Teresa had given away their food money.

These sisters of the poor didn't neglect the sick of Moti Jihl or Tiljala. One couldn't. They were everywhere in Calcutta. But Mother Teresa always needed medicine. On one trip to beg medicine, she asked Michael Gomes

WORLD EVENTS OF 1952:

Curly Howard, of *The Three Stooges* fame,
    dies at age forty-eight.
The Diary of Anne Frank is published.
First successful surgical separation of
    conjoined twins is performed.
Cheez Whiz is introduced.

to go with her. She showed him a long list of drugs she
needed.

"It's hopeless," he said, but he accompanied her anyway.

At a large pharmacy, she showed the manager behind
the counter her list. He reddened. "You've come to the
wrong place, lady!"

She took her appeal to a higher court. She sat down
right in the store and began praying. Let God decide. Behind the counter the manager watched her, growing more
exasperated every minute. Suddenly, he burst into a frenzy
of activity. He came to her lugging several packages.

"Here are your medicines! Now please leave."

"God bless you."

"Consider them a gift from our company," he sputtered.

Some of the sick overwhelmed the senses. One man
had been so weakened he was unable to protect himself.
Flies had laid eggs in his wounds. One of his limbs was
being eaten by maggots, the larvae of flies. The sight was

disgusting beyond endurance. The stench was nauseating. Mother Teresa felt faint as she pulled the wiggling white larvae loose. She had to get every last one, too, then scrape the wound and disinfect it. She reminded herself that helping the man was like helping Jesus.

When the man was cleansed and bandaged, Mother Teresa said to her novices, "If I didn't believe with all my heart and soul that this man's body is the body of Jesus, I couldn't bear such an abomination for one second."

The essence of her commission was summed up in two words: "I thirst." Mother Teresa was convinced that the Lord pleaded for love for the least of the least. As a reminder to the members of the order, the words "I thirst" hung over the sisters' crucifix on the wall at Creek Lane.

After a novice had ministered to one of the destitute, one so repulsive that normal people could not bear to look, let alone smell such a person, Mother Teresa would take the novice's hand, palm out. One by one she would fold the novice's fingers and thumb back into the palm as she said the five words, "You did it to Me."[1]

Over the weeks, more novices appeared. God was astonishing Mother Teresa with His bounty. Mother Teresa's drawing power seemed too strong for some to believe. They said so. But she reminded herself to think nothing of it. It was not her power. It was the power of Christ that was drawing these workers. Jesus was the source of all her power, her strength. She was no social worker. Every poor person she helped was like helping

Christ. Jesus, in the book of Matthew, said it better than she ever could:

> *Then shall the King say unto them on his right hand, Come, ye blessed of my Father, inherit the kingdom prepared for you from the foundation of the world: for I was an hungred, and ye gave me meat: I was thirsty, and ye gave me drink: I was a stranger, and ye took me in: naked, and ye clothed me: I was sick, and ye visited me: I was in prison, and ye came unto me. Then shall the righteous answer him, saying, Lord, when saw we thee an hungred, and fed thee? or thirsty, and gave thee drink? When saw we thee a stranger, and took thee in? or naked, and clothed thee? Or when saw we thee sick, or in prison, and came unto thee? And the King shall answer and say unto them, Verily I say unto you, Inasmuch as ye have done it unto one of the least of these my brethren, ye have done it unto me. (25:34–40 KJV)*

At Creek Lane, Mother Teresa and her girls expanded on the third floor, even though they slept side by side on mats. First one room and then another was filled by the new workers. Mother Teresa governed them strictly. At 4:40 each morning, she rang a hand bell, calling cheerfully, "Let us bless the Lord!"

"Thanks be to God," the sleepy sisters responded.

Mother Teresa rang a bell when they were to pray,

when they were to eat, when they were to leave the house, when anything was to happen on their grinding schedule. Her bell only brought smiles to their faces. After all, so far they were all former students of hers. Wasn't Mother Teresa the very same sister and taskmistress who had rung the bell when they were to step under the shower? Rung the bell when they were to soap up? Rung the bell when they were to rinse off? Rung the bell when they were to dry off? Not to mention the bottle of permanganate of potassium she thrust at them so they would be sure to gargle!

As yet they had no chapel. They attended services in Saint Teresa's, pastored by Father Henry. Why bother the Gomes family for room for a chapel? Mother Teresa's one year outside the convent was almost up. Suppose the archbishop said, "Well, you tried, but it's not going to work"? What if their work was all for nothing? Mother Teresa had not even written the rule or constitution for her order yet. But when did she have time? In the meantime she and her girls ventured forth every day, always in pairs, to help the poor.

"It is wise to send them in pairs for safety," commented one well-meaning observer.

"It has nothing to do with safety," answered Mother Teresa in her usual blunt way. "It is the Lord's will for His servants in Luke 10. He 'sent them two and two before his face into every city and place, whither he himself would come.'"

When would Mother Teresa's lay friends and helpers learn that her decisions were not made to accommodate this world? At times she may have seemed to accommodate the world, but her real guide in all things was the Lord.

"Give wholehearted and free service to the poor," she reminded her girls again and again.

In 1949, life was almost normal again for India, if one could accept crushing poverty and ever-present disease as normal. Mother Teresa decided she must show her confidence in the new India, which was led by one of Gandhi's protégés, Jawaharlal Nehru. Mother Teresa became an Indian citizen.

Soon after, when Michael Gomes accompanied her on a streetcar, she sat patiently, hands folded in the Hindu way, listening to Bengali gossip swirl about her. "This little foreign woman is trying to convert Hindus to Christianity," someone hissed in Bengali. This foreign woman was trying to do this. This foreign woman is trying to do that.

Finally, she smiled. *"Ami Bharater Bharat Mar,"* she said softly in Bengali.

"I am an Indian, and India is mine,"[2] Michael repeated proudly in English.

But then Calcutta was devastated once again, this time by politics. Pakistan, the new Muslim country to the east that bordered the city of Calcutta almost on its eastern boundary, closed its borders to trade with India. No longer could Calcutta depend on the raw jute produced in the great swampy delta of the Ganges River. The soft lustrous fiber from the great fourteen-feet-long stalks was used to manufacture twine, paper, and burlap. It was a major industry for Calcutta. Jobs, which were hard enough to find anyway, dried up by the hundreds of thousands. Mother Teresa's calling seemed more vital than ever. Yet would her fledgling order survive? In August her year was up. God would decide.

One day in August 1949, her spiritual adviser, Father Celeste Van Exem, told her dryly, "His Reverend Archbishop thinks it would be a shame to disband these girls."

"Yes, they've worked so hard. Some of them even studied at night so they could finish their degrees at Saint Mary's. Still, if it's God's will. . ." Mother Teresa waited patiently.

"You do have your ten novices, I believe?"

"Yes. A couple of them left, but more came. Praise God for that."

"You can in the future maintain at least ten sisters for a congregation within our archdiocese, I suppose?"

"God willing."

"The archbishop is going to Rome in April of next year. If you had your constitution ready. . ."

Mother Teresa worked feverishly on the constitution of her order. The main difference between her order and other orders was a fourth vow: to "give wholehearted and free service to the poor." And of course her girls were not cloistered. They had to go directly to the poor.

Father Van Exem reviewed her first draft to make

sure it violated no canon law. When he had made his revisions, he took it to the official canonist for the diocese. The canonist reviewed every little detail. After all, they couldn't embarrass their own Archbishop Perier, who was going to personally deliver it to Cardinal Pietro Fumosoni-Bondi, the head of the Propagation of Faith at the Vatican!

The diocesan canonist read the opening words of Mother Teresa:

> Our object is to quench the thirst of Jesus Christ on the cross by dedicating ourselves freely to serve the poorest of the poor, according to the work and teaching of Our Lord, thus announcing the Kingdom of God in a special way.
>
> Our special mission is to work for the salvation and holiness of the poorest of the poor. As Jesus was sent by the Father, so he sends us, full of his spirit, to proclaim the gospel of his love and pity among the poorest of the poor throughout the world.
>
> Our special task will be to proclaim Jesus Christ to all peoples, above all to those who are in our care. We call ourselves Missionaries of Charity.
>
> "God is love." The missionary must be a missionary of love, must always be full of love in his soul, and must also spread it to the souls of others, whether Christian or not.[3]

"This endeavor has the finger of God on it!" gushed the canonist.

Mother Teresa had her mind on God but her feet on the ground. She spoke with many Loreto sisters and many Jesuit priests. Several told her a story that amazed her. When the archbishop heard a certain priest had told a sister of Loreto that Mother Teresa was being tricked by the "wiles of the devil," the archbishop called the priest in and confronted him. When the priest confirmed he had said Mother Teresa was being tricked by the devil, the archbishop ordered him to apologize to the sister of Loreto.

The story was out. All professed religions in Calcutta now knew what the archbishop thought of brothers and sisters who made difficulties for Mother Teresa. If her calling was truly from God, something very wonderful might be growing in her little order at Creek Lane.

"It seems the archbishop is not going to let anyone trample your Missionaries of Charity," said the sisters of Loreto.

Father Van Exem put an advertisement in the Calcutta *Statesman* soliciting donations for Mother Teresa's work in Moti Jihl. Gifts were to be sent to the church he pastored. The very first donation was delivered by car. It came from none other than Dr. B. C. Roy, the chief minister of Bengal! He had been Gandhi's last physician. Nehru entrusted Dr. Roy with Bengal, a most difficult province of the new India. Because Bengal was choked with refugees from Pakistan, their chief minister had

When He was dying on the cross, Jesus said, "I thirst." Jesus is thirsting for our love, and this is the thirst of everyone, poor and rich alike. We all thirst for the love of others—that they go out of their way to avoid harming us and to do good to us.

to be a man of great compassion. Nehru had picked the right person for the job. It was said Dr. Roy actually gave free medical service to needy patients in his medical office every morning before leaving to tackle his government work.

"You may have a powerful friend here in Dr. Roy," Father Van Exem told Mother Teresa. "He's a member of Brahmo Samaj, a sect that believes in only one God and abhors idol worship. He's more sympathetic to Christians than most government officials."

On October 7, 1950, the Missionaries of Charity became an official order within the diocese of Calcutta. By then, twelve sisters were with Mother Teresa. Part of a large room on the third floor of the Gomes house was now a chapel. Early one morning His Grace, the archbishop himself, celebrated its first Mass. The decree was read by Father Van Exem, who began:

For more than two years now, a small group of young women under the guidance of Sister Teresa, a lawfully uncloistered religious of the Institute of the Blessed Virgin Mary, have devoted themselves. . . .[4]

He went on to expand on their vows, especially the fourth, that set them apart:

> *To fulfill our mission of compassion and love to the poorest of the poor we go:*
> * *seeking out in towns and villages all over the world even amid squalid surroundings the poorest, the abandoned, the sick, the infirm, the leprosy patients, the dying, the desperate, the lost, the outcasts:*
> * *taking care of them*
> * *rendering help to them*
> * *visiting them assiduously*
> * *living Christ's love for them and awakening their response to His great love.*

After the service the celebrants sat down at a long table for breakfast. Among the guests was Sister Cyril, representing the Medical Mission Sisters in Patna. Sister Cyril was not able to down the required four chapatis of Mother Teresa's order. Chapatis were thin pancakes of unleavened bread.

"You see, we don't eat just rice and salt," Mother

Teresa told the chastened visitor. "We must keep our sisters strong."

"And what is the daily schedule for your sisters?" asked Sister Cyril.

"We rise at 4:40. We have prayers in common at 5:00. Mass is at 5:45. Every day. Then after our breakfast of chapatis and tea and various household duties, the sisters leave the house to go to the poor. At 12:30 they are back for lunch. Then they rest—nap, if they wish—and pray. From 2:30 to 3:00 are reading and meditation. Then tea at 3:15. From 3:15 to 4:30 is adoration of the Blessed Sacrament—"

"Oh yes," interrupted Sister Cyril enthusiastically, "fervent prayer before the bread of the Eucharist is so important!"

"Adoration of the body of Christ is all the more important for our order," continued Mother Teresa. "After that, once again they go forth to the poor until 7:30. Evening prayers are at 9:00 and blessed bedtime at 9:45."

The archbishop inspected Mother Teresa's living quarters with the wide eyes of an owl. "Even sleeping side by side in dormitories, your days here at Creek Lane are numbered, Mother," he observed. "I'll speak of it to Father Van Exem and Father Henry."

Over the next two years, the number of sisters grew to more than twenty. They had the entire upper floor and part of an adjacent building owned by the Gomes family. The Gomes family insisted they loved having Mother

Teresa and her sisters there, especially after supper when the girls laughed and sang for an hour. What greater music was there than the tinkling laughter of young ladies?

How shocked outsiders would have been to see Mother Teresa herself, hands on waist, doubled up with laughter. Otherwise, the sisters were so disciplined one hardly knew they were there except for her ringing bell. They even padded up and down a back wooden stairway as silently as cats.

"Silence is of utmost importance in training novices," Mother Teresa explained to Michael Gomes when he mentioned it to her.

"Silence?"

"Yes. The religious need silence to hear God speak to them."

Silence is so important, she thought. How could one overestimate its importance? There could be no life of prayer without silence. Silence of the eyes, the ears, the mouth. Silence let prayer lead to love and kindness. Love led to humility. Humility brought joy of serving God. And a sister, no matter how poorly she felt, could not forget the joy of the risen Christ if she always tried to think of Christ. That was why it was so important to think always of Christ. Love. Humility. Joy. But first, silence and prayer. It sounded mystical to the nonreligious, but it worked as flawlessly as God's physical laws for the universe.

In 1952, Mother Teresa had a very unexpected visitor. It was so sudden. Never had she expected to see several automobiles pull up by the Creek Lane house. From them flooded ecclesiastical purple. Bishops. One was Bishop Perier. Then red. A cardinal!

Soon Bishop Perier was introducing Mother Teresa to Cardinal Francis Spellman from America. The cardinal had been visiting American soldiers in Korea. He had stopped in Calcutta. But what was a cardinal doing at Creek Lane? Was Bishop Perier so proud of her little order?

"Follow me, Your Eminence," she said to the cardinal, a plump man with glasses that sparkled like spotless crystal.

She took the cardinal to a very large room on the upper floor of the house. It was full of tables and benches. "This is our refectory now," she said, referring to their dining hall.

"Where is the rest of your convent, Mother?" asked the cardinal, puzzled. "Where do you sleep?"

"In many small rooms on this floor and in here, too. We push the tables and benches to the side." She continued matter-of-factly, "This room is also our study room, and at the end behind that partition is our chapel. In short, this floor of the house is our convent."

The cardinal smiled, then walked to the end of the room to celebrate Mass for the sisters in their chapel.

Later, one of the sisters ventured, "Don't you think His Eminence looked surprised, Mother? He must have been wondering how we can accommodate any more sisters." The sister's face revealed she wondered the same thing.

"God will provide for us," agreed Mother Teresa, as unperturbed as always.

But something did perturb her very much. It was a problem that transcended sickness. It was no less than death itself. Yes, death. The religious talked much of a good death. That was death for them after a life of obedience to God. But on the streets of Calcutta, Mother Teresa saw death in its most brutal, heartless form. People died unnoticed, uncared for. Of course it afflicted the very people she served: the poorest of the poor. One day, while walking with Michael Gomes not far from Creek Lane, she saw a man lying by the roadside very near the Campbell Hospital.

His pulse was a faint tap. "This poor man is very close to death," she said. "Let's get the hospital to take him in."

"We cannot accommodate him," the attendants at the hospital answered vaguely.

Mother Teresa scurried after medicine. When she returned to the man, he was dead. She rushed to the commissioner of police to vent her indignation. They had crossed paths before.

Before she could tell him why she was there, he said, "Some people were in here a few days ago complaining about you again. Get rid of that meddling European woman, they demanded. I said, 'Certainly, if you will get your wives and daughters to do the work she and her sisters are doing now.'" He smiled. "That always shuts them up. No one ever wants to do the heartbreaking, backbreaking work you do."

"I tried to get a dying man into the hospital," she said, brushing off the praise. "They wouldn't take him. Now he's dead."

"What am I to do? I don't have the authority to force them to take people with no money at all. You know we police often take such people in an ambulance to a place run by Dr. Ahmed, our health officer. But we don't have the resources to pick up everyone. Good grief, Sister, who knows how many die in the streets of Calcutta every day?"

"From what I've seen, thirty or forty every night."

"One thousand a month!" His calmness evaporated.

"People would not allow their dog or cat to die on the street like that!" she cried.

Mother Teresa left the commissioner. He was a good man. The seed had been planted. Perhaps something good would grow. He had helped her in small ways before. When certain hooligans or goondas threw rocks at her, they soon stopped after a word or two from the commissioner's policemen. "Leave the good lady alone; she is not foreign at all, but an Indian citizen like you."

In the meantime, Mother Teresa knew exactly what had to be done about the people dying in the streets. She and her sisters would take them in. But they needed a shelter. And that would require prayer. In force.

"We shall pray for that—a shelter for the dying—and a new house for you, too," she told the sisters.

Every evening Mother Teresa and the sisters walked with Father Henry in a procession all the way to his church of Saint Teresa. From there they walked to Fatima Chapel, a small open chapel erected by Father Henry. All the while they said aloud the Rosary or other prayers. Then they returned to the house on Creek Lane. The effort took three hours. The sisters were already very drained from their normal work. Yet they persisted. Day after day. Week after week.

" 'I can do all things through Christ which strengtheneth me,'" Mother Teresa reminded the sisters, as well as herself.

Meanwhile the problem of the dying would not go away.

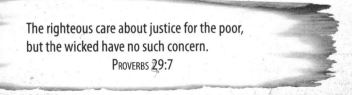

The righteous care about justice for the poor,
but the wicked have no such concern.
PROVERBS 29:7

9

HOUSE OF THE DYING

Death pervaded the poor streets of Calcutta.

Mother Teresa simply could not look the other way. Sometimes she was so desperate after finding a dying man or woman that she spent what little money she had hiring a taxi or rickshaw to take the wasted body from hospital to hospital until one would take the poor soul.

Sometimes after a refusal she would remain on the hospital steps, hoping to shame them into taking the dying. Occasionally that worked, as it did once with a woman half eaten by rats and ants. If it did not work, all she could do was give her love and care until the victim's last breath.

But the problem would not go away. She rented a cheap room in the slums and began caring for the dying there.

Then Mother Teresa visited Calcutta's health officer. They gave each other *namaste*, the Hindu greeting of respect with palms pressed together. She had done that for many years. She explained what the Missionaries of Charity were doing with the dying, and added, "Our small room will soon be overflowing."

"We can't take care of all the dying, either," he admitted. "We barely remove their corpses before they turn to dust." Then he lamented, "This is a great dishonor to India."

"Our Missionaries of Charity can do it. But we must have a larger shelter."

"There is a place, but it's much too far from Moti Jihl."

"Perhaps not."

"It's by the Kalighat." He shrugged.

"The Temple of Kali!"

"Yes." He shrugged hopelessly again as if the temple was much too far away. "There's a large enclosure by the temple. It was originally a *darmashalah*, a resting place for pilgrims to the temple. But now it's been taken over by the goondas, the hooligans, for drinking and gambling and worse. Too bad it's so far from Creek Lane."

Yes, the temple was a long way to the south from Creek Lane, but Mother Teresa was excited. What a comfort it would be for her Hindu patients. The temple was the very place they would wish to spend their waning moments. And the space was actually a caravansary, a resting place for pilgrims. How well she knew those. One of the finest caravansaries in all Europe was right in Skopje. The *Kusumli Han* was hundreds of years old, an enormous two-storied structure with the distinctive alternating brick and native stone.

The memory excited her. "Show the darmashalah to me," she gushed. "Please."

In his car, the health officer explained the Hindu story that when the goddess Kali married the god Shiva, her father, King Daksa, was enraged. Her father organized a sacrifice in which Kali was thrown onto the flames. Too late Shiva came to rescue her. Holding her burnt body, the bitter husband began a dance of cosmic destruction. All the other gods appealed to Vishnu to stop Shiva. Vishnu came but had to hack Kali into fifty-one pieces to tear Shiva away from her. According to legend, a toe off her right foot fell where this particular temple was built. People were cremated at ghats at the Temple of Kali. Of course, explained the health official, Calcutta got its very name from Kalighata.

"Goats are sacrificed daily south of the temple," he added helpfully.

Mother Teresa was aware of the custom. Years ago around the temple she had asked what stained all the foreheads rusty red. Goat's blood, someone answered. As they approached the Kalighat, its presence was heralded by its huge silver dome, scalloped on the bottom. Fluted onion-shaped domes jutted up on the corners of a lower structure. The air was sharp with incense and funeral smoke.

The vicinity was choked with small shops and street vendors serving the temple. Beggars. Garish flowers. Tourists. Caged birds. Religious prints. Miniature shrines. Images of the countless Hindu deities. Not only were vendors and pilgrims milling about in every conceivable garb, from silk to the cheapest cotton weave, but hundreds of priests bustled around the temple, too. Amid the teeming life was death. Funeral processions plodded slowly by.

The health officer opened the door of the car. "This way, Mother."

Mother Teresa followed the health officer behind the temple to walk into a yawning elongated room. A spacious aisle separated areas of concrete raised on both sides for sleeping. The health officer walked through the room into a passageway. Then another elongated room opened up just as large as the first!

"What do you think, Mother?" asked the official.

"God bless you."

Mother Teresa could scarcely believe such a blessing from God. The ample dormitories were perfect. They were even wired for electricity, although any native of Calcutta knew power was often too weak to light the smallest bulb, especially in days of summer heat. But there were connections for gas, too. If that were not enough, there was even a small courtyard. *Praise God for answering the unceasing prayers of the sisters,* Mother Teresa thought. Such a huge answer, too!

Very wretched-looking men were lying about. They had the surly look of goondas. She smiled at them. The rooms were trashy and smelled foul, but the filth was just as temporary as the goondas.

"There may be resistance to you Christians settling right next to the temple," said the health officer uncertainly.

"Some always resist us."

"There will be rumors you are converting them into Christians in their dying moments."

"We do convert people. We convert Hindus into better Hindus. Muslims into better Muslims. Besides, respected Indian officials like yourself or the police commissioner can inspect us if you like. And it wouldn't hurt to put your conclusions in the newspaper to allay suspicions. If you wish, of course."

"Doesn't anything discourage you?" He smiled, pleased. This would make his job easier. His health department couldn't keep up with the dying. It shamed the city. "I'll tell the police commissioner the Missionaries of Charity are now taking the darmashalah for a house of the dying. I'm sure he'll want his policemen to give a friendly word or two to the goondas."

"God bless you. We'll be here tomorrow to clean it."

Within twenty-four hours it had all been arranged. The sisters arrived, armed with buckets, ammonia, mops, rags, and brooms. The goondas were gone. Bottles and refuse soon flew out of the two huge dormitories. After that the sisters swept then scrubbed the floors and walls. It would be known as *Nirmal Hriday*, Mother Teresa told her sisters, which was Bengali for "Place of the Pure Heart."

Nirmal Hriday opened August 22, 1952, just four days before Mother Teresa turned forty-two. Every morning the sisters looked for the destitute dying, often hidden under piles of rags, often flagged by a swarm of flies. Soon every sister knew that such people could easily be carried to a rickshaw by two sisters. The dying weigh so little.

So the dying were brought to Nirmal Hriday, not only by the sisters, but by the city's health department. It was not long before dozens of dying people were lying on the raised areas on mats. The first ward entered was for men. The second more private ward was for women, who came in almost equal numbers. There was no shortage of dying in Calcutta. In the connecting passageway, under shrouds, were those who had not survived the night.

Many, like the health officer, called it the "House of the Dying." The only concession Mother Teresa had to make to city officials was not to admit lepers. Harboring the dread disease in the very heart of Calcutta at a sacred temple would enrage the locals and frighten away the pilgrims.

Some people protested anyway. "You should be killed yourself," they screamed at Mother Teresa.

"I would go to God sooner," she answered fearlessly.

Some protesters were coaxed inside. The protests

dried like sand in their throats. Hospital smells of medicine and human waste clogged the nostrils. On mat upon mat stretched cadaverous bodies in soft light from high overhead windows.

Mother Teresa well knew that once accustomed to the smells, a visitor succumbed to the eerie peacefulness of the death wards. Every sound was muted. Sisters floated from poor soul to poor soul, cleaning them, feeding them, consoling them. Most were beyond saving physically. After all, they were only admitted if the hospitals refused them.

But they could be saved emotionally. How it wrenched the heart of every one of these poor wretches to know not one soul on the face of the earth cared enough to lift their dying body off the grimy street. But then they were picked up! Soft hands stroked their forehead with unreserved love. Yes, it was a Missionaries of Charity. Love.

"I came in here the most miserable wretch in creation," sobbed one old man. "Now I'm going to die like an angel."

Men and women were almost equally afflicted. Wasted to nothing. Tuberculosis. Cholera. Cancer. Old age. Lunacy. Occasionally the dying person was a child. And because of their infirmities, the victims were all starving to death when they arrived.

Mother Teresa knew a few could be saved. But at first it would be very few. And the others were ministered to with loving care as they drew their last breaths. They were indulged by the sisters whenever possible. Often it was a treat

they hadn't had in years. Grapes. Candy. A cigarette. Then
they slowly drifted into death. Rescue had come too late.

The few who were Christians or Muslims were taken
away to be buried in an appropriate cemetery. If Hindu,
as most were, they were carried to the nearby ghats to be
burned.

Occasionally in the first days the peace was shattered.
"How dare the authorities turn this darmashalah over to a
Christian woman?" screamed one typical intruder.

The most persistent protests came from Hindu priests
assigned to the Temple of Kali. Then one of these very
Brahmins was struck down by tuberculosis. He failed
rapidly. To his utter dismay, the hospitals refused him.
Everyone abandoned him. He was at death's door.

Calamity of calamities, he was taken to Mother Teresa's House of the Dying. At first he raged against it. But the love of the sisters overpowered his bitterness. Soon he was as sweet and content as the others.

His dignified demise was not lost on the consciousness of other Hindu priests. They observed that his body was sent to the ghats for his last Hindu rites. Their protests became halfhearted, then died.

"These kind sisters seem to be love in human form," some of them whispered.

The priest was not different than many who were brought in. One Christian was an articulate Englishwoman, an elderly teacher who had a long run of bad luck. "Got a cigarette?" she asked with her remaining breath. She wore an ironic look on her tired face, as if to say, *It could happen to you, too, you know.*

But the vast majority of the dying were Hindu and Muslim. A few were unconscious and never identified. For their funeral it was assumed they were Hindus.

As Mother Teresa walked the aisles, she seemed surrounded by a sea of all manner of humanity. Men. Women. Some in agony. Some comatose. Some barely conscious, wheezing their last breaths. Some were ancient. Some mere youths. Some were hideous-looking, great tumors pulling down one side of their faces. Some seemed made of sticks. "Jesus in His distressing disguise" was what she reflected. Most reached for her. At death's door, they longed for the touch of a kind hand.

She couldn't pass anyone without stopping to respond. "God will care for you. He loves you," she whispered.

Often Mother Teresa realized the weak, withered hand was trying to comfort her! Compassion among the dying for each other was stunning. If the wards were full, some would give up their mat to a newcomer who appeared to be suffering more. Many were even smiling. At last someone cared for them. Peace at last. Some smiled because they grew stronger. They would recover. At the rate they were being brought in and at the rate they left, either dead or recovered, Nirmal Hriday would be a place of comfort for over one thousand poor souls a year. All who entered the wards, dying or otherwise, quickly realized the solemnity, the importance of the place. How paramount it was to bring a person peace before he or she met God.

"After all, they are passing on into eternity," realized most visitors with shock.

Mother Teresa knew that at some point she would have to start a Nirmal Hriday in Moti Jihl that would serve mostly Muslims. But it was while the sisters were putting love into full service at Nirmal Hriday that Father Henry told Mother Teresa a very large house on Lower Circular Road had been found. It seemed that the archbishop had sent him and Father Van Exem on their bikes to search all over east Calcutta for a suitable house for the new order.

"It might be a good motherhouse," said Father Henry.

"Describe it, Father," she asked.

And as Father Henry began to describe the house, she realized she knew which one it was. She had walked down Lower Circular Road many times. One had to take that busy street to reach the Sealdah railway station. The house was very plain from the outside, but in size it was more like a hotel. It was four stories high and wider than it was tall. In her mind Mother Teresa quickly estimated the huge house offered maybe ten times the space the sisters now occupied.

"It's too big," she interrupted.

"Not at all." Father continued, "It's the home of a wealthy judge, a Muslim named Doctor Islam, who decided he wants to move to Pakistan. The judge feels like he is giving it away. But still, I suspect it will cost over a hundred thousand rupees."

"More than a hundred thousand! But where will we raise such money?" asked Mother Teresa. "We have a tiny amount, but it is for essentials like medicine."

"The archbishop told me the diocese will advance you the money for it," answered Father Henry. "If the price is right."

Later Mother Teresa learned Doctor Islam had been deeply disappointed in the amount of the offer. "It's barely more than the land is worth," he gasped to Father Van Exem. Doctor Islam had been so overcome, he had rushed off to a mosque to pray for guidance. And perhaps he asked a few of his friends about this Mother Teresa, this minuscule woman in the blue-bordered sari. "Does she really help one and all?" When he returned, he had tears in his eyes. He shrugged. "God gave me this house. I give it back to Him."

In February 1953, the twenty-eight sisters of the Missionaries of Charity moved from Creek Lane into their new motherhouse at 54A Lower Circular Road. Their tiny order was now deep in debt to the diocese. The imposing structure on close examination seemed more like three buildings clustered around a courtyard. Yet no large entrance opened to the street.

The entrance was along a narrow alley. There, hidden in dim light, were two tall doors painted black and heavily bolted at the top to the door frame, at the bottom to the concrete slab, and in the middle to each other. Soon, by the entrance there hung a chain beside a sign reading, "Mother M. Teresa MC." A pull on the chain rang a bell and summoned a novice. Directly inside the entrance was an alcove that opened into the large, tiled courtyard.

Mother Teresa smelled temptation. "Many religious orders have started out serving the poor, only to later end up serving the rich and taking on more and more trappings for themselves. We must guard our poverty, which after all is a choice we make and a holy vow."

So she made sure the grand new surroundings had no effect whatever on the sisters' poverty. Their only possessions remained a metal bucket for washing, a thin sleeping mat, and their clothing. They had two habits: one to wear, one to wash and dry. They needed only two because the cotton fabric was so coarse it dried very fast. In addition to their tunics and saris, they had rough underwear, sandals, and the crucifix they pinned to their left shoulder. Although their new motherhouse was enormous, the sisters would all sleep in one dormitory. Did not the poorest of the poor sleep packed together like sardines? Entreaties by well-meaning visitors to add small luxuries like fans were resisted strongly by Mother Teresa.

"Do the poorest of the poor have such luxuries?" she asked.

Amenities in the motherhouse remained few indeed. If the poor didn't have something, the sisters didn't have it, either, except for a decent diet and clean clothes. The sisters had to keep up their energy and their hygiene.

But even the kitchen was austere. The sisters were not allowed to cook on anything but a charcoal fire, just as the poorest of the poor did. No toaster, no oven, no stove. No washing machine. No radio. No generator as backup during all the frequent electricity blackouts. In the alcove by the entrance, Mother Teresa might allow a chair, even a fan, but those were only for waiting visitors.

Mother Teresa pondered the subject of a telephone. "I can certainly see it might be useful to ring up some government officials rather than travel all the way across Calcutta in a streetcar to talk to them."

She agonized. She didn't normally worry about money. It seemed to come. But she did worry about wasting money. Her benefactors sacrificed things they wanted for themselves to give her money. Would it be a waste to get a telephone? It seemed to her not to fit their vow of poverty. But if she spent more money on streetcars to talk to people than the phone would cost her to talk to the same people, then wasn't she wasting money? It was a big decision.

"For the time being, we will not have a telephone," she announced.

Outside the motherhouse, the sisters were not even allowed to accept a cup of tea on the hottest day. They quenched their thirst from water in an old plastic bottle they carried with them in a cloth bag. After four years of working in the slums in their white saris, the sisters of the Missionaries of Charity were becoming widely known for not accepting food or water outside the convent.

It was also becoming known that, besides what they wore on the street, they owned one other sari and almost nothing else. When they had moved from Creek Lane to the new motherhouse, it had taken each sister no more than one minute to roll her extra habit inside her sleeping mat. Their poverty was real, very real. The poorest of the poor realized that. For this reason and from the deep respect all Indians felt for holy people, they were never molested. A goonda might shout an insult, but even a goonda would not think of attacking a sister.

Government officials began to contact Mother Teresa about training their workers to work with the poor. "Teach us your technique. What special kind of sociology do you use?" Even the Communists pestered them: "What is your secret? Why do the poor listen to you and not us?"

She shrugged. If only she could tell them. But how could she convince people who didn't believe in God that service to every poor person she met was service to Jesus Himself? How could she convince them her strength came from Jesus? It was not unusual for her to be asked to take over some government project that sputtered. One official even asked her to take over four homes in Calcutta that the city ran for vagrants. She weighed the request very seriously.

"Oh, how I hate to refuse such a good project," she told her spiritual adviser. "But it would require most of my sisters."

And what a great event approached for four of her sisters!

Live in harmony with one another. Do not be proud,
but be willing to associate with people of low position.
ROMANS 12:16

10

"CHRIST LIVETH IN ME"

One month after the Missionaries of Charity moved into the motherhouse, the initial four sisters of the order took first vows for a professed sister at the nearby cathedral of Our Lady of Rosary. These vows would be given twice a year: on a feast day of Mary. For this first time, Mother Teresa took the vows, too. Archbishop Perier and several priests conducted the service. After the gospel reading and sermon, one of the priests called each of the five sisters by name.

Each answered, "Lord, You have called me."

"My dear Sister, what do you ask of God and His church?" asked a priest.

"I ask that I may follow Christ my spouse and persevere in this religious community until death," responded the sisters.

The priest explained that each sister had already been

consecrated to Christ by baptism. This profession aimed at holiness. Now they wished to be even more closely bonded to Christ, so that all they did and said, thought and desired, might be only for His glory.

"Dear Sister, are you resolved to unite yourself more closely to Christ by the bond of perpetual profession?"

"I am so resolved," they all answered.

"Are you resolved with the help of God's grace to follow the life of perfect chastity, obedience, and poverty that Christ our Lord and His virgin mother chose for themselves and to persevere in it forever?"

"I am so resolved."

"Are you resolved, by the grace of the Holy Spirit, to spend your life in wholehearted free service to God's poor?"

"I am so resolved."

"Are you resolved to strive constantly for perfect love

of God and your neighbor by zealously following the gospel and the rule of this religious community?"

"I am so resolved."

Then after the entire congregation prayed that the sisters would be faithful to God's call and their vows, each sister said in turn what Mother Teresa said. From the document of her profession she read, "I, Sister Mary Teresa, vow for life chastity, poverty, obedience, and wholehearted free service to the poorest of the poor according to the constitution of the Missionaries of Charity. I give myself with my whole heart to this religious community so that by the grace of the Holy Spirit and the help of the Blessed Virgin Mary I may seek to practice perfect charity in the service of God and the church."

The priest told each sister in turn, "By the authority entrusted to me, I accept your vows in the name of the church for the community of the Missionaries of Charity. I commend you earnestly to God that you may fulfill your dedication, which is united to His Eucharistic Sacrifice."[1]

Each sister went in turn to the altar, leaving the document of her profession, which was united to the communion that followed.

At the time of communion, Paul's words in Galatians were sung: "I am crucified with Christ: nevertheless I live; yet not I, but Christ liveth in me. . . ."

And thus the first sisters of their order were professed.

Soon the Missionaries of Charity had their own chapel in the motherhouse. It was a large room lit by daylight coming in windows on the wall facing Lower Circular Road. There were no pews or chairs. Worshippers sat and kneeled on the floor, with or without jute mats. Their altar was a table at one end. Behind the altar on the wall was a crucifix with the all-important words: "I thirst." Off to the side was a statue of Mary, the mother of Jesus.

Although professed sisters were few, Mother Teresa had worked out a schedule for service. New girls were accepted as aspirants. They would spend six months coming face-to-face with the poorest of the poor and the dying before they became postulants. At the end of one year of mostly studying church history, theology, and scripture, the postulants would become novices. First-year novices did field work among the poor only on Thursdays and Sundays. The rest of the time they were very busy in the motherhouse receiving rigorous spiritual training.

"Naturally the priests must guide us spiritually," said Mother Teresa.

Besides conducting services every day, the priests kept a sharp eye on the postulants and novices. No one was more watchful than Father Henry, who instructed them daily in spiritual matters. Nor was anyone more frank. If Father Henry saw a novice, even a professed sister, not saying prayers as she walked the streets of Calcutta, he would be sure to let her know she was falling short of her calling.

"Father Henry tells them things no one else tells them," said Mother Teresa with satisfaction, because she knew Father Henry knew just how hard to reprimand a novice without discouraging her. He had a gift for instruction.

Second-year novices worked among the poor like professed sisters, every day but Thursday. On Thursday they and the professed sisters were in the motherhouse attending to housekeeping. They scrubbed the house and spent time mending their habits, as well.

Thursday was a day for fun, too. Often the women were taken on picnics. Other times they stayed in the motherhouse and made candy, danced sacred native dances, and taught each other hymns, both Christian and Indian.

Trips to the outside were now measured in precious minutes from the motherhouse. It was twenty or so minutes to Kalighat by streetcar. On foot it was about twenty minutes north along Lower Circular Road to Saint Teresa's and Father Henry. Going that same direction, it was twice that long to Baithat Khana and Father Van Exem.

It was also about forty minutes off to the northeast to the Loreto compound or Moti Jihl. Mother Teresa certainly hadn't forgotten the needs of Moti Jihl. Perhaps if she went directly to see this Dr. Roy, the chief minister of Bengal, she could at last get a water well drilled. Then the poorest of the poor could get good clean water from a pump.

"Why have I delayed my request so long?" she scolded herself.

As if she were a patient herself, she waited outside Dr. Roy's medical office at six o'clock in the morning. Finally, he made his rounds. She worked with sick people enough to know he was diagnosing patients with extraordinary speed and skill. He was a massive, towering man. Although seventy years old or so, his slicked-back hair was black. His face was intent, yet dark eyes loomed gently behind thick horn-rimmed glasses.

"And what is your problem, madam?" he asked her.

"I am Mother Teresa of the Missionaries of Charity."

"Sounds familiar. What is your problem?"

"Moti Jihl needs a water pump. With clean water much of the cholera can be prevented."

"No water pump in Moti Jihl?" he asked in surprise. He turned to his assistant. "Make a note to see about this woman's complaint." He turned to Mother Teresa, who was already getting up to leave. "And how is your health, Mother?"

"God has blessed me."

She returned again and again, always waiting patiently with the needy. She asked Dr. Roy for electrical hookups, water connections, garbage removal—all the basic things of civilized society—and always for the neediest neighborhoods. Every time he would ask his assistant to look into it. And every time something was actually done.

Finally, Dr. Roy knew her too well. "You again, Mother Teresa? You have too much to do for the needy to wait around like this. I can't have that. From now on you

MOTHER TERESA ON THE HOME:

We must remember that love begins at home and we must also remember that the future of humanity passes through the family.

come directly to my office at the Writers' Building on Lall Bazar Street in the afternoon. Walk in straightway."

Mother Teresa continued to rule her order. In her own mind, as mother superior her most important duty was to train sisters and recruit them. She still stayed up late every night writing letters. Nothing she saw could ever let her stop such long days. Sometimes she slept no more than an hour or two. But why waste this wonderful gift of life, this wonderful service to Christ, on sleep?

In return the Lord gave her strength. The sisters themselves concentrated on the growing schools for children in Moti Jihl and on the House of the Dying at Kalighat. Much effort was required to move the dying off the streets.

"Let's do something beautiful for God," Mother Teresa often told the sisters.

So much more needed to be done. Mother Teresa needed a center for dispensing medicine. It would replace the makeshift dispensary at Saint Teresa's. Pairs of sisters roaming the streets were not efficient at dispensing medicine, because they invariably became occupied with the dying or hungry. She reasoned that the motherhouse could not be used for such a purpose or the flow of activity into and from the house would become hopelessly clogged. If and when medicine was dispensed, there still remained the matter of food. The poorest of the poor were desperately hungry. And then there were the babies...

"Don't ever let a baby die," she pleaded to anyone who would listen to her. "Let a Missionaries of Charity take it."

Yes, one could not forget the most innocent of the poor. The sisters found babies every day in the arms of dying mothers—even in trash heaps! People felt they could not afford to raise the little ones. The poor innocents, looking like tiny papered skeletons, usually died within hours after they were found. But a few lived. The sisters had the tiny twig-limbed survivors scattered about Calcutta with this family and that family. Some of the babies even became chubby after a while. If only Mother Teresa could do something bigger for the abandoned babies.

In 1955 one of the sisters at the motherhouse told her, "A man stopped by to say there is a very large house for rent right on Lower Circular Road—within walking distance of here."

Soon Mother Teresa and the sister were striding on their way. In five minutes they saw a huge two-story house, once white but now the ubiquitous soft pink hue caused by the red dust of Calcutta. Around the house was an enormous fifteen-foot wall interrupted only by metal gates eight feet high. The gates opened wide enough for a truck to pass through into a large dusty courtyard.

"This great house has great possibilities!" exclaimed Mother Teresa.

Her mind was churning. This was more than she had hoped for. Not only could the house take babies and children, but it could serve the poor in other ways, as well.

"Nirmala Shishu Bhavan," she said with no hesitation, "the Children's Home of the Immaculate."

She rushed to the Writers' Building to see the chief minister of Bengal. She was allowed to walk straight into his office. Dr. Roy had told her the truth. He put his work aside.

"Would you like some tea, Mother?" he asked.

"Our order does not accept food or drink outside the motherhouse," she answered gently. "Would it be possible to get some food and medicine from the government to distribute to the needy?" she then asked without hesitation.

He promised to look into it. She mentioned the babies. He seemed especially interested. What was their condition? How were they treated medically? How many survived? Where did they come from? Who were the mothers? Which neighborhoods had the greatest problems?

"Do you think we sisters are tackling too much, Dr. Roy?" Mother Teresa asked out of politeness. She had no intention of backing down.

"Not at all. Make it bigger. Bigger, Mother. A good cause never suffers for want of money!"

What faith Dr. Roy had. It was as great as her own. Soon she rented the house. Five thousand rupees a month would have made her hesitate a few years earlier. But now if everything except having the money in hand was acceptable in a venture, she always forged ahead. It seemed each effort brought more money trickling in. Once someone made the mistake of suggesting she invest some of the money they received.

Mother Teresa was shocked. "Our money is to spend on the poor! Do you expect them to wait?"

Not only would this large new house shelter babies, but it would also serve as a distribution center for as much food and medicine as contributions would buy. Soon people congregated outside the new house every morning, wanting medicine or clutching empty pots of brass and tin.

Muslims were served one day. Hindus another day. Mother Teresa knew that mixing the two groups was not wise.

Many of the people coming for food and medicine were not the most destitute of Indians, but she could no longer ignore hardworking people whose wages bought them shelter and only three weeks' worth of food every month. Therefore, workers began cooking rice in huge metal vats in the dawn hours, only a short time before the gates opened to the hungry with their outstretched empty vessels.

"America has a great surplus of wheat," hinted one visitor.

"These poor people can't use wheat or wheat flour," answered Mother Teresa. But later she learned that wheat could be shipped and stored in a form called bulgur if it was parboiled first. It was a method thousands of years old. Then the bulgur could be cooked just like rice. Maybe she could talk to Dr. Roy about it.

Feeding the hungry was very important, but the heart of Shishu Bhavan was the first floor of the house. There cribs began to fill with babies. Some infants seemed comatose, but many blinked and blubbered as the sisters bustled about them. Toddlers played on the floor. Some of the children were three or four years old. A few were barely able to walk, even at that age. They suffered from tuberculosis and rickets, the latter causing curvature of the spine and limbs.

But a few children, except for the pain of being unwanted, seemed unscathed. There always seemed to be one precocious child, not much more than a toddler, who acted like a regular little mother, busily wiping noses and scolding the others.

There was vicious gossip about Shishu Bhavan at first. All babies were baptized as Christians, said the rumor-mongers. But the reputation of the sisters was strong now. They walked into the slums all the time. The slum dwellers knew the sisters did not convert. All they did was urge one and all to pray.

As the word spread that some very healthy infants were being raised by the sisters, well-to-do Indians began to step forward to adopt them. The sisters still had to silently endure heartbreaking prejudices that favored boys, fair skin, good health, pretty faces. But at least those poor babies would have a chance at a decent life.

Because some parents wanted to keep adoption a secret, the baby was taken to a nursing home where its new mother "delivered" the baby, then left with it after a suitable time.

"Mother," said one of the sisters, "I know of a few teenage girls in Moti Jihl who are orphans. Men prey on them. They're made to sell their bodies to survive."

"You must invite them here, of course."

Some of the poor orphan girls were pregnant. No one ever raised the possibility of abortion a second time to Mother Teresa. Abortion was the greatest abomination known to man, she would scold. It was against God, against nature, against mankind, against children, against women. It was the death knell of humankind.

"If a society allows a mother to murder her own child, what is left of that society?" she demanded to know.

Some of the babies died, but none met God without knowing first that they were greatly loved. Mother Teresa had a plan for those who could not be adopted, especially the disabled. They would be schooled. And if they lacked the intelligence for school, they would be taught a simple trade.

"And what kind of dowry can we give the girls when they marry?" pondered Mother Teresa aloud.

"Dowry!" exclaimed one of the sisters. "Are you planning so far ahead?"

"A sari, a ring, a few little things," muttered Mother Teresa. "Somehow we will find dowries for them. We must pray."

Just as Dr. Roy urged, Shishu Bhavan became larger and larger. So did the rest of the order's enterprises of mercy. The sisters visited the slums daily, ran their schools, ran dispensaries, distributed food, and cared for both the children and the dying. There was nighttime duty, too. Although Nirmal Hriday was often entrusted to responsible hired help for the night, Mother Teresa insisted only sisters remain at Shishu Bhavan overnight. Precious infants must remain in their constant care.

Some of the religious who did not work with Mother Teresa began to ask, "Just how long can Mother Teresa and her Missionaries of Charity keep up this pace?"

But Mother Teresa only planned more activities. "We need a mobile clinic to carry help to the poorest of the poor," she told Eileen Egan from Catholic Relief Services when asked what her most pressing need was.

And with money from Catholic Relief Services in New York and from the Reverend Scheider in Delhi, a van was purchased and renovated into a medical clinic. It was called "Mother and Child Clinic." The van kept a regular schedule in six slum areas in and around Calcutta.

Mother Teresa always tried to accompany the van

> ## MOTHER TERESA ON GIVING:
>
> It is very important for us to realize that love, to be true, has to hurt. I must be willing to give whatever it takes not to harm other people and, in fact, to do good to them. This requires that I am willing to give until it hurts. Otherwise there is not true love in me, and I bring injustice, not peace, to those around me.

to its Kidderpore location south of Calcutta. This was a Muslim district. The only way Muslim men would allow their women treatment was to be assured the sisters or a woman doctor was administering the medical treatment. The presence of Mother Teresa assured them everything was just as it should be.

It was at this site that one little boy was found to be suffering from red worms, parasites so hideous they could swarm up though the esophagus and block breathing! He was rushed to Shishu Bhavan where he made a full recovery.

In 1957, Mother Teresa had to at long last face one of Calcutta's most dreaded problems: leprosy. Five lepers came right to the motherhouse. How could she resist a direct appeal from the most reviled of the reviled? Gobra, the one leper hospital in Calcutta, had been shut down. Even Dr. Roy would not help Mother Teresa keep it open. It was better for lepers to be kept out of Calcutta, he insisted.

Before long, Missionaries of Charity were using a van to service locations solely for lepers on the outskirts of Calcutta. By 1958 the number of locations had grown to eight. Some estimated that thirty thousand lepers lived in the Calcutta area.

"They live by begging, since no one will employ them," said Mother Teresa. "On Sundays they slip into Calcutta and beg around Christian churches. On Friday evenings they work Muslim mosques. Of course they are also around Hindu temples. But they don't dare remain long at these places. When begging is no good, they move back into their various enclaves in the slums."

Mother Teresa learned a lot about leprosy. Leprosy had been dreaded in India since time immemorial. The youngest children heard the symptoms discussed in a tone of stark horror. An area of skin became numb to the touch. Numbness spread. The numbness led to frequent injuries and infections because the patient felt no pain from small accidents. Eventually came the classic signs that stamped a poor victim a leper: loss of fingers and toes, perhaps even the nose. Another sign was the repulsive "lion face," a large bloated face with nodules welted up under the skin.

"Lord, have mercy on our ignorance," cried Mother Teresa. "The cause of leprosy has been known since 1874. For years the disease has been treatable with the oil called chaulmoogra. Now we have new drugs far superior to that."

Mother Teresa's bright blue mobile van would pull up to a storage shed at one of the locations solely for lepers. Helpers unlocked the shed to gain access to patient files. A doctor or a sister trained in tropical medicine began to inspect the lepers who lined up. Two sisters cleaned the patient's infected areas as the doctor examined the patient and noted disfigurements on a diagram of a human figure on a stiff file card.

With few exceptions the patient was given the drug called Dapsone or DDS. This new drug was very effective but so potent it had to be administered gradually. An overdose could cause severe nerve damage. Still, with early treatment the patient could escape with no permanent injury at all.

"You must realize," Mother Teresa reminded those who feared the disease, "it is also vitally important to the community that the medical team render the patient noninfectious, no matter how badly disfigured the poor soul might be."

By 1958 the sisters of the Missionaries of Charity numbered eighty-six. Shishu Bhavan cared for about one hundred children, and the same number were provided for in the House of the Dying. About half of the destitute who had been brought in dying, recovered, and each year the recovery rate improved.

The sisters ran fourteen slum schools that served hundreds of children. The Corporation of Calcutta was now firmly behind Mother Teresa, furnishing a building when she had a steady one hundred pupils at any one location. The teachers had blackboards and ample supplies. There was even a shiny new water pump at Moti Jihl by the stagnant pond. Now the poor had clean water.

And Mother Teresa never relented in her effort to supply milk to the poor, too. All unfortunates got milk: babies, children, mothers, lepers. The mobile leper clinics were treating well over one thousand lepers. The next year the sisters planned to open a large dispensary for lepers in Titagahr on the outskirts of Calcutta.

The order of Missionaries of Charity was almost ten years old. Had the order really proven to provide dynamic love among the poorest of the poor? Would the archbishop ever want the order to set up houses outside the diocese of Calcutta? Or were other areas even interested in these sisters who served the poorest of the poor?

"God knows," said Mother Teresa obediently.

> I have been crucified with Christ and I no longer live, but Christ lives in me. The life I live in the body, I live by faith in the Son of God, who loved me and gave himself for me.
> GALATIANS 2:20

11

THE POPE

Yes, Mother Teresa was obedient. For years she had paid little attention to Vatican politics. But that changed in 1958. Who could ignore the events in Rome? Pope Pius XII, who had shepherded Roman Catholics since 1939, died in October.

Pope Pius was succeeded by the almost unknown archbishop of Venice, Cardinal Angelo Roncalli. Rumors were that Roncalli was at least seventy-six, sleepy-eyed, and fat. God forbid the gossip, but who didn't think he was just a caretaker pope?

"Cardinal Montini, the logical successor, has been deemed by the College of the Cardinals as a bit too young yet," gossiped some. "Our new holy father, God bless him, will reign at most five to ten years." Implied in the words was the assumption nothing was going to happen in the church for five to ten years. All progress in the church was on hold!

Archbishop Perier was himself eighty-three. He made it plain to all the religious in Calcutta how he felt about this new pope. "Is John XXIII conservative?" asked the archbishop rhetorically. "Or is he liberal? He is both. And God will speak through him."

And in 1959, the archbishop had words for Mother Teresa alone: "Although you now have nearly one hundred sisters, Mother, your order of the Missionaries of Charity still isn't officially ten years old." He paused. "But there is no harm in probing the possibilities of an area or two outside Calcutta ahead of time."

"Thank you, Your Grace."

Mother Teresa immediately boarded a train to Chota Nagpur. Many of the Hindi-speaking sisters of the Missionaries of Charity had come from that rugged high country west of Calcutta. Its forests were interrupted by many precipices and highlighted by tumbling waterfalls. Wildlife was that of legend: tigers, elephants, pythons, leopards, and bears.

In the more cultivated areas around Mahuadan and Noatoli, the parish priest, Father Harrison, promoted Mother Teresa's efforts tirelessly. Once he sent ten candidates to Calcutta at one time. Early on he had offered the Missionaries of Charity a house with a garden and a well at Daltonganj. But the archbishop had squelched the offer. At that time, it had been too soon to venture outside the diocese of Calcutta.

Hurtling toward Chota Nagpur, Mother Teresa had much time to reflect that the archbishop dearly loved her order. He wanted a preview of things to come. After all, he would retire in 1960, the very year her order would be ten years old.

His retirement was part of an ongoing process in the church started by Pope Benedict XV. For forty years the church had diligently implemented Benedict XV's encyclical to develop native clergy and native bishops. In 1960 the diocese of Calcutta would at last have an Indian cleric.

This fact reminded Mother Teresa that Pope John XXIII had just called for a great Vatican council to promote spiritual vitality, Christian unity, and world peace. Father Van Exem told Mother Teresa it would be open to nearly three thousand bishops, and that for the first time in history, such a meeting would be attended by predominantly non-Europeans and natives of the lands they served as bishops. Hundreds of Catholic theologians and even non-Catholics were also being invited to observe.

"It seems His Holiness is not the inactive old care-taker after all," Mother Teresa told herself with some satisfaction. "It seems our archbishop was right. God is speaking through this old pope."

She also reflected on what had happened in India itself over the past ten years. With the "Muslim problem" behind them—whether they liked separation from Pakistan or not—the Indian Constituent Assembly, under Jawaharlal Nehru's strong leadership, had endorsed a new constitution. India was formally proclaimed a republic on January 26, 1950. One clause of the new constitution outlawed untouchability. Another instituted the right for women as well as men to vote in future general elections.

"At long last every Indian has a future," Mother Teresa mused. "Even the poor—God willing—with our help."

To no one's surprise, the congress had elected Jawaharlal Nehru prime minister. Nehru was a Gandhi disciple who had pulled away from the Mahatma near the end. He was not a committed pacifist but coldly pragmatic. He was of the highest caste, a Brahmin of Kashmir. He was arrogant and so English in manners that he joked about being the last British viceroy. Still, he was articulate and probably the one Indian in India able to bridge the India of the British Raj and the India of Indian rule.

Ironically, in its first year as a republic, India suffered several natural disasters: a drought in southern India and severe earthquakes and floods in Assam. Relief from the rest of the world was slow in coming because Nehru refused to accept relief with political strings attached. He opposed India taking sides in the political struggle between Communism and the Western democracies.

Eventually India benefited from this neutrality, as aid poured in both from the Communists, especially the Union of Soviet Socialist Republics, and from the Western democracies, primarily the United States. By 1959 India still maintained neutrality, although the Communists of Red China were constantly threatening their common border.

"None of that will deter the Missionaries of Charity," reflected Mother Teresa.

In 1960 she opened a house in Ranchi, a city of several hundred thousand at the east edge of Chota Nagpur. She had only proceeded after being invited by the bishop of its diocese. She resolved never to barge into an area, only to discover the bishop resented the presence of her sisters. No, the bishop must want her sisters there. He must ask for them. Other conditions had to be met, as well. First, the sisters must work only among the poorest of the poor. Second, they must never be so overworked that they had no time for prayer. Third, a priest of solid doctrine and virtue must be there to act as their spiritual adviser and to celebrate Mass for them. Last, Mother Teresa must have at least six sisters available to operate the house.

"In a pinch, we might do it with five," she admitted reluctantly.

In what Mother Teresa hoped might become routine, several sisters packed their simple belongings before they departed on the train to begin the house in Ranchi. Before the departing sisters left the motherhouse, the other sisters sang hymns to them. As they loaded their bedrolls and buckets into the van outside the motherhouse, the order prayed for them. By the time they had finished loading supplies for the poor, Mother Teresa was just finishing the prayers.

The sisters headed for Ranchi were joyous. Through the birth of Jesus, Mary had brought joy to the world. Now through their love of Jesus, they would bring joy to the poor. At the Sealdah railway station, the sisters carried their load to the train: bedrolls, buckets, blankets, bags of food, and cardboard boxes full of supplies.

This was just the first new venture that year. Within one year, Mother Teresa opened houses in three other cities, all within the eyes of the central Indian government at New Delhi: Delhi, Jhansi, and Agra. The city of Delhi had special poignancy for Mother Teresa. Inauguration of the new house drew several dignitaries, including Prime Minister Nehru himself, now in his seventies and frequently very sick.

In dealing with secular authorities Mother Teresa never forgot her Master. She said to the dignitaries, "Let us first go and salute the Master of the house."

At the chapel she knelt in prayer. Prime Minister Nehru stood at the back and made a polite *pranam* with folded hands. Krisha Menon, Nehru's most trusted political friend, examined the altar and asked Mother Teresa what certain inscriptions meant. Then they held the ceremony. Poor children, who were being schooled by the sisters, honored the prime minister with garlands of flowers. Then they knelt and prayed in unison.

"They offered prayers and small sacrifices to God to obtain His graces for you," explained Mother Teresa to Nehru. "Sir, shall I tell you about our work?"

"No, Mother, you need not tell me about your work. I know about it. That is why I am here. Take good care of these children. One day one of them may be prime minister."

Mother Teresa suspected he knew of her work through her acquaintance with his daughter, Indira Gandhi. Indira acted as the prime minister's hostess because Mrs. Nehru had been dead for many years. But Indira was much more than a charming hostess. At forty-three, she was a skilled politician. With Nehru's health failing, more and more Indians speculated he would be succeeded by Indira. This meant that Mother Teresa was known to the highest secular powers in India.

The year 1960 continued at a dizzying pace. Novices came from England, Germany, America, and Malta. So did an invitation from the National Council of Catholic Women in America.

Mother Teresa consulted the archbishop. "Surely you will not want me to go to America to speak publicly to these women, will you, Your Grace?"

"It's a perfect opportunity for you to stop in Rome on your way back to India and present your petition for pontifical recognition of your order. Not to mention the financial support for your order you will generate from other countries."

"But I won't ask them for money."

"Just tell them what you do, Mother."

In October, Mother Teresa flew alone from Calcutta to Las Vegas. There she met the three thousand delegates of the National Council of Catholic Women. Apparently Bishop Edward Swanstrom, head of Catholic Relief Services, had been the catalyst for her invitation. But one of the first to welcome her in Las Vegas was Cardinal Cushing from Boston.

"Welcome to America, Mahatma Gandhi," he said to Mother Teresa, joking but also with great respect.

Such a sinful place as Las Vegas for the site of the convention did not surprise Mother Teresa. After all, why shouldn't Catholic women visit such a debauched place? Did Jesus shy away from sinners? Perhaps there would be a little less sin after they left. Meditating in the desert outside of Las Vegas before her talk, Mother Teresa gathered thorns from a cactus and twisted them into a crown.

"This will be my souvenir of America," she told the woman who drove her. "At our motherhouse in Calcutta I will put it on the head of Christ on our crucifix."

When the time came for Mother Teresa to speak, she

was nervous about addressing such a large audience. But she was not fearful. That betrayed a lack of trust in God. She closed her eyes and made a cross on her lips with her thumb. It was her fervent appeal for Christ to speak through her. She did not use notes, yet she had thought a great deal about what she might say. She believed that to be completely unprepared and cross her lips was not trusting God but rather being presumptuous.

Mother Teresa avoided looking at individual faces. But as she spoke to the sea of faces, her nerves calmed. She told anecdotes of the poor. Her emphasis was their own heroism: brave mothers, so weak themselves, who trudged wearily to the clinics, bearing their children.

At the end of her talk she said, "We Missionaries of Charity depend on the providence of God. We don't beg. All we say to Hindus and Muslims and Christians is 'Do something beautiful for God.'"

After the talk Mother Teresa sat at a booth answering questions. She had nothing with her but the cheap cloth bag every sister of her order carried into the field. Many a woman that day decided to forgo a sumptuous dinner and do something beautiful for God. They gave their enter-tainment money to Mother Teresa and the poor of India. She had to empty her bag into another hastily obtained container many times. She collected thousands of dollars.

Mother Teresa made stops all across America. In Peoria, Illinois, she personally thanked the Catholic women who had been supporting her Mother and Child

> ## MOTHER TERESA ON ADOPTION:
> Please don't kill the child. I want the child. Please give me the child. I am willing to accept any child who would be aborted and to give that child to a married couple who will love the child and be loved by the child. From our children's home in Calcutta alone, we have saved over three thousand children from abortion. These children have brought such love and joy to their adopting parents and have grown up so full of love and joy.

Clinic in Kidderpore, south of Calcutta. She told them that in 1959, six such clinics treated seventy-four thousand Indian mothers and children! She made stops in Chicago and Washington, D.C.

In New York, she visited many well-known Catholics: television commentator Bishop Fulton Sheen, a warm, brilliant man; Bishop Edward Swanstrom, head of Catholic Relief Services; Dr. Marcolino Candau, director of the World Health Organization; and Dorothy Day, the controversial social reformer.

On a side trip to Connecticut, Mother Teresa visited Indian Christians who had a child dying of leukemia. "Return the Lord's love," she counseled the parents, "even though the sign of His love is this cross you must bear."

All across America she had witnessed enormous

wealth and vast fields of grain. Yet lying on the streets of New York she saw the destitute, some poor, some sick, some drunk. America's great wealth had not solved all of its problems.

From New York, Mother Teresa flew to London. In London she visited the Indian ambassador, a television interviewer, an old friend from India named Ann Blaikie, and various powerful individuals connected to relief agencies. She continued on through Europe, meeting similar movers and shakers. Her trip was providing her with dozens of contacts who might later help the poor in India, just as the archbishop had told her.

By mid-November 1960, Mother Teresa reached Rome. This city was, to her, the mountaintop. First of all, she saw her brother! Was it possible she had not seen Lazar in thirty years? Lazar, now fifty-three and working for a drug company, lived in Palermo with his wife, Maria, and ten-year-old daughter, Agi. The years rolled away as Mother Teresa saw her brother: still tall, lean, and militarily erect.

"Oh, Lazar!"

"Gonxha! Oh no, I must call you Mother Teresa now." He grinned.

Mother Teresa did not speak Italian, and her Albanian was very rusty. But they managed to share sadness over the fates of Mama and Agatha. Albania was now the most rigid, the most backward Communist country in the world. It disdained any contact with Western democracies. It was hard for Lazar to believe its dictator Hoxha had been a military cadet with him in Tirana. The acquaintance with Hoxha did Lazar no good at all. His only direct contact with Mama and Agatha was the exchange of a few letters.

"Let us sing some old Albanian songs," enthused Lazar, noticing how difficult conversation was.

So they sang and joked.

It was good Mother Teresa talked to Lazar before going to the Vatican. Could any Catholic be prepared for the exhilaration of that experience? Her heart soared when she first saw the grand dome of Saint Peter's Cathedral. The dozens of statues sculpted by Gian Bernini that topped the colonnade hinted of its vast piazza. Her first stop was near Saint Peter's to see Archbishop Franjo Seper, a Yugoslavian.

"So this is the little person I have been hearing so much about," he said to her.

Such praise made her uncomfortable. The glory was God's, not hers. But the praise did not disturb her as much as it might have in any place other than the Vatican. It was not hard to be humble amid its immensities. When she strolled through the interior of Saint Peter's Basilica, she realized the inside was more colossal than the outside. Its vastness held ten thousand worshippers during special papal masses.

The artistry was staggering. Coiled and bronzed pillars towered above the high altar. This huge canopy, the *baldacchino*, was also designed by Bernini, the mastermind

MOTHER TERESA ON THE UNITED STATES:

If we remember that God loves us, and that we can love others as He loves us, then America can become a sign of peace for the world. From here, a sign of care for the weakest of the weak— the unborn child—must go out to the world. If you become a burning light of justice and peace in the world, then really you will be true to what the founders of this country stood for.

of Saint Peter's Piazza. The giant marbled and bronzed Chair of Saint Peter in the apse of the church was his work, too. If that were not enough, Bernini also designed tombs for the popes, as had Michelangelo earlier.

The genius of Michelangelo was also present in the basilica. Not only did he sculpt the intensely moving pietà, but he also had a hand in designing the exterior dome of Saint Peter's.

And now I am to have my greatest moment of all, Mother Teresa thought as she was admitted to the papal palace. For Mother Teresa was being allowed to attend a Mass celebrated by the pope himself.

She was ushered into the Sistine Chapel. Her companion explained that the enormous fresco of the Last Judgment on the altar wall was by Michelangelo. The saved ascended to heaven everlasting on one side; the damned descended into hell eternal on the other side. High overhead on the vast ceiling, Michelangelo's frescoes captured the grandeur of the Old Testament: God Separating Light from Darkness; the Creation of Adam; the Creation of Eve; the Temptation; the Fall; the Flood; the Patriarchs; the Prophets; in fact, all that preceded the coming of Jesus.

"It seems the swirling panorama leads one's mind straight to God," whispered her companion.

Suddenly, Mother Teresa realized the pope was entering: Pope John XXIII. Her awe turned to sympathy. The pope seemed to labor under his weighty vestments. Nearly eighty years old and quite heavy, Pope John was to celebrate Mass for the Dead in memory of prelates who had died during the previous year.

"*Requiem, aeternam dona eis, Domine: et lux perpetua luceat eis. . . ,*" began the pope. *Eternal rest give to them, O Lord: and let perpetual light shine upon them. . . ,* thought Mother Teresa as the pope spoke the service in Latin.

After the service, as John XXIII was leaving the chapel, he passed by Mother Teresa. She stepped forward to kiss his ring. The pope paused to gaze at her, then blessed her. Mother Teresa stepped back, unabashed. She might never get a chance to see a pope again as long as she lived. The Gospels were full of stories of people who rose from the multitude to seek personal contact with Christ. Did he ever reject them? Did they ever regret their action?

"*Madre fondatrice,*" whispered clerics in Italian as she

was whisked to her next contact in Rome at the Piazza di Spagna.

"Mother of the poor," translated a friend who was with her.

Mother Teresa met with Cardinal Agaginian and Archbishop Sigismondi of the Sacred Congregation of the Propagation of Faith. There she presented her petition to make her order pontifical. This would allow her to set up houses in other countries. Such a request usually was not granted until an order had proven itself for thirty or forty years. But Mother Teresa was already fifty years old. Her order was just ten years old. Could she wait such a long time? And didn't the poorest of the poor need help in other countries?

The cardinal quizzed her about how the sisters were trained. He was astonished by what the order had accomplished without outside funding. It did seem very providential. The two ecclesiastics read the order's prayer book. The little book was cheap and poorly reproduced but legible. Its very shabbiness seemed to greatly affect the two clerics. Who could not know Mother Teresa and her sisters denied themselves everything but the barest of necessities to do something beautiful for God?

Finally, Mother Teresa flew home to India.

For the Lord loves the just and will not forsake his faithful ones. They will be protected forever.
PSALM 37:28

12

A SERVANT LEADER

In India the praise of Mother Teresa continued.

In 1961 her good friend Dr. Roy, still active, paid her a great compliment. Newspaper reporters asked him what he was thinking about on his eightieth birthday. His reply was front-page news in the Calcutta *Statesman*: "As I climbed the steps of the Writers' Building leading to my office, I thought of Mother Teresa, who devotes her life to the welfare of the poor."

That same year, the Missionaries of Charity added two houses. One was in the town of Ambala in the Punjab, north of Delhi. The Punjab, an area of climatic extremes—stifling hot to bitter cold—was also an area of turbulent passions. Many battles between armies had been fought in its dusty plains and mountain passes. But was the potential for violence any reason for Missionaries of Charity not to help the poorest of the poor? Mother Teresa didn't think so.

The other house was created in Bhagalpur on the south bank of the Ganges River in eastern Bihar. Bihar was familiar territory for Mother Teresa. Just upriver on the Ganges was Patna, where she had received medical training.

In 1961 the sisters, now numbering 130, also opened a mobile leper clinic in Bengal at Asansol, where Father Van Exem now pastored. Asansol was the very place Archbishop Perier had sent Mother Teresa back to in 1947 during her waiting period. It jolted her occasionally to realize Archbishop Perier had retired. Still, the new archbishop, Albert Vincent, gave her free rein.

The government helped Mother Teresa more than ever. Late in 1961, the Missionaries of Charity acquired thirty-five acres of land from the government. The land was two hundred miles from Calcutta and fifteen miles beyond Asansol. This would be the future site of a leper town, where lepers could live in peace while they received treatment.

"We will call it *Shanti Nagar*," said Mother Teresa, as if the Town of Peace were an accomplished fact.

Mother Teresa also initiated another idea that year. Some of the work of the Missionaries of Charity was simply too demanding for women. So she began to explore the idea of an order of Missionary Brothers of Charity. There were many things to be worked out. It could not be headed by a woman. And there was a new archbishop. Would he support such an effort?

She appealed to Father Van Exem. "Would you be so kind as to discreetly explore the issue with the archbishop?"

In 1962, the sisters opened a house in the province of Maharashtra that hugged the west coast of India. Its chief city was Bombay, but the house was far in the interior in Amaravati. Nevertheless, it was a big step outward from Calcutta. The language base of this province was neither Hindi nor Bengali but Marathi. And in September, Mother Teresa was called by Prime Minister Nehru to Rashtrapi Bhavan, the presidential palace in Delhi. There she was presented with the Padmi Sri Award for service to India. The atmosphere was splendid, with colorful palace guards, and at first very formal, with sober-faced dignitaries.

"Good heavens, then the crowd cheered and clapped, even stomped their feet," she said afterward. "Perhaps my humble habit reminded them of Gandhi."

Travel was taking more and more of her time, especially long train trips to her houses all over India. Travel on Indian Air, the domestic airline for India, was too expensive. So she approached a government official. "Perhaps I could earn my way each trip by working as a stewardess," she suggested in complete sincerity.

The official stared at her in disbelief, apparently trying to visualize the tiny fifty-two-year-old nun pushing a tray of tea and soft drinks down the aisle. "I don't think so," he concluded.

Mother Teresa never gave up easily. She kept asking. Her request must have filtered higher and higher in the government. Did it ever finally reach Prime Minister Nehru or his daughter, Indira Gandhi? She did not know, but one day an apologetic government minister called to assure her she would get a certain number of free passes on both Indian Air and the government's international carrier, Air India. Her service as a stewardess would not be required.

Her extensive travel had another effect. She was not at the motherhouse enough to be the strong mistress of the novices that she had always been. That duty could not be neglected. So Sister Agnes, her first recruit, became mistress of novices. About this time a new priest replaced Father Henry as spiritual director of the novices and postulants. He was Father Edward Le Joly.

October 1962 was the beginning of a forum for good works that was better attended than any other in the history of the Catholic Church: the Second Vatican Council. Several bishops praised the godly work of Mother Teresa, not the least of which was the papal nuncio to India in New Delhi, Archbishop James Knox.

The enthusiasm for her work had now spread far beyond India. Many countries with seemingly intractable problems with the poor asked for the presence of this miracle worker. A bishop in Venezuela especially wanted her order. But of course the Missionaries of Charity could not go outside India until the pope made it pontifical. Mother Teresa already knew that often took thirty to forty years!

"This pope does not do everything so slowly as some other popes have done," speculated some of the religious community in Calcutta optimistically. Mother Teresa didn't worry about the issue. She took hold of the work that already faced her order.

During 1962, the border confrontation between China and India intensified. Both countries added outposts along the frontier territory in the Himalayas. In October the Chinese attacked Indian outposts on both western and eastern parts of the border. The attack ended only when Beijing announced a cease-fire in late November. The Indians had been humiliated enough.

After fifteen years, Nehru's flirtation with the Communist world ended. To satisfy his critics, he got rid of his defense minister, who happened to be Krishna Menon, his closest political friend.

In 1963 the Missionaries of Charity opened three more houses in India: Patna, Raigahr, and Bombay. The latter west coast city prided itself as the gem of India. It boasted many mills and wealthy neighborhoods. It was the one diocese to which Mother Teresa had to write and volunteer the services of her sisters. The bishop accepted her offer, but many wondered if a house would have been started there without Mother Teresa's offer.

Mother Teresa knew bishops had to exercise great diplomacy with their own constituents. So if she made it possible for the bishop to accept without angering prideful locals, why should she care? Even at that, Mother Teresa's presence in Bombay was not appreciated by everyone. And her candid comment that the slums of Bombay were worse than those of Calcutta stung the pride of Indians in Bombay. How dare this woman criticize Bombay! How dare she compare Bombay to Calcutta!

She answered with knowledge of the poor unknown to the upper class. "Calcutta's slums are single-storied, sprawling. The children have ventilation, some space. In Bombay the people are stacked atop one another in tenements. Ventilation is poor. Space is minimal. Water is very hard to get."

One great development in 1963 was the foundation of the Missionary Brothers of Charity. Its head would be a tall, thirty-eight-year-old Australian priest of the Society of Jesus. Originally Ian Travers-Ball, he was called Brother Andrew. The Jesuit had his own ideas, too. Although Mother Teresa wanted a religious habit for the brothers, Brother Andrew did not.

"And so their constitution will state," Mother Teresa

told the sisters, "that the brothers will wear the clothes of the poor people, but they will be always clean and neat. In India it will be a shirt and trousers. The sign of their profession and dedication to Christ will be a simple crucifix worn over the heart."

"You said 'In India,' Mother!" gasped one sister. "Surely it will be many years before the brothers can serve in other countries."

"We must look to the future."

Although some of the original brothers were priests, no new brother would be accepted if his intention was the priesthood. The vows and the training of the brothers were closely like those of the sisters, but their special call was to serve Jesus in ways that demanded more physical strength.

It was not long before the first fledgling brothers, including Brother Andrew, managed to buy a house in Kidderpore. They were especially helpful to the sisters with lepers at Titagarh and with the men's ward in the Home of the Dying. But they also began work with the toughs of the street: derelict men and roughneck boys. Boys in particular needed guidance before they grew into hardened goondas. That required not only present care but also hope for the future. So the brothers became quickly involved in vocational training.

"We will teach them to repair things like radios," Brother Andrew told Mother Teresa.

Mother Teresa was stunned by news from Yugoslavia in

July of that year. Skopje had been devastated by an earthquake. In its dim past, she recalled, it had been leveled by earthquakes, as well. The Emperor Justinian had rebuilt the town about AD 530. But no such earthquake had before happened during her lifetime.

The news from Yugoslavia became progressively worse. Over one thousand people were dead in the rubble. Many of the buildings of the town had collapsed. What irony. Often she had wished Mama and Agatha had remained in Skopje instead of being marooned in Albania, now a desolate Communist wasteland. But if they had remained, would they now be buried under rubble? Had God sent them away? Would she ever learn not to doubt God's guiding hand?

Another stunning development in 1963 was the death of Pope John XXIII. The surprising old pope had served not even five years, but his legacy would be enormous. The Second Vatican Council was recommending major changes in the liturgy and habits. Gone in many instances were the use of Latin and traditional habits. Laypeople would have much greater participation, too. Another major emphasis of the council was tolerance toward other religions.

There was no reason to think the new pope, Paul VI, would not advocate these major changes. As Cardinal Montini, he had been an active participant in the council. And he quickly showed he was favorably disposed toward India, too.

Maybe in our own family we have somebody who is feeling
lonely, who is feeling sick, who is feeling worried, and these
are difficult days for everybody. Are we there, are we there
to receive them, is the mother there to receive the child?

"To think the holy father is coming here next year,"
said Mother Teresa when she heard the news.

Pope Paul VI visited Bombay for the Eucharistic
Congress the following year. Archbishop Knox had encouraged it. The great surprise to Mother Teresa was that
the pope had decided to give her the brand-new white
convertible that had been furnished him by Americans in
India. It even became a press event as Paul VI presented
it to her in a small ceremony.

Mother Teresa's special recognition by the pope was
more than she had ever dreamed of. It was even disturb-
ing. Many now treated her as some kind of celebrity.
Of course she wasn't disappointed in the pope. He had
a much greater problem with such misguided attention
than she did. But the attention bothered her.

She shrugged it off and wasted no time in raffling
off the huge Cadillac or Lincoln Continental or whatever make it was. It earned her Missionaries of Charity
460,000 rupees. Of course the money had to be used for
the poor.

MOTHER TERESA ON SHARING:

Some time ago in Calcutta we had great difficulty in getting sugar. I don't know how the word got around to the children, but a little four-year-old Hindu boy went home and told his parents, "I will not eat sugar for three days, I will give my sugar to Mother Teresa for her children." After three days his father and mother brought him to our home. I had never met them before, and this little one could scarcely pronounce my name, but he knew exactly what he had come to do. He knew that he wanted to share his love.

"And the sooner the better," said Mother Teresa. "We will not have manna for the poor sitting in a bank."

On May 27, 1964, Nehru, prime minister of India since its independence in 1947, died. He was succeeded not by his daughter, Indira Gandhi, but by Lal Bahadur Shastri, formerly Nehru's home minister.

Mother Teresa continued to open new houses throughout India: familiar Darjeeling in Bengal; the booming steel town of Jamshedpur in south Bihar; historic Goa on the west coast where the sisters were actually entrusted with the chapel of Saint Francis Xavier; and equally historic Trivandrum of Kerala, further south on the west coast. The area around Trivandrum, the southern tip of India, was associated with the apostle Thomas!

The sisters of the Missionaries of Charity numbered over two hundred. Few ever left the order. Now the Missionary Brothers of Charity were following the lead of the sisters, more slowly but steadily. Few brothers or sisters ever succumbed to the dread diseases they worked with. But occasionally one fell victim.

In 1964 Sister Leonia, who headed the house in Raigahr, came to the motherhouse in Calcutta for a meeting. Mother Teresa noticed her glazed look immediately.

"You don't look well at all," Mother Teresa told her bluntly. "Are you getting enough rest?"

"I have a very sore throat," Sister Leonia replied, betraying deep worry with a look of anguish.

Within hours, Sister Leonia was racked by spasms in her chest and throat. A fever and dry cough sent chills into Mother Teresa's heart. Could Sister Leonia have what Mother Teresa thought she had? *Please, God, no.* She rushed Sister Leonia to the hospital. On the way she learned the sister had indeed been bitten by a dog. The sister had cleaned and cauterized the wound. That was a fatal mistake. But there was no point in admonishing her now.

The doctor confirmed Mother Teresa's suspicions. "The sister has rabies, Mother. There is no known cure on earth for it at this stage. As you know, the treatment must be taken right away. I'm very sorry, but I'm afraid the end will be very painful for the sister."

And so it was. Mother Teresa told Sister Leonia frankly what had happened, then remained with her as she twisted in agony, rocked by convulsions and delirium. Just as Mother Teresa received Sister Leonia into service for Christ, she now tried to comfort her as she passed on to Christ.

The extreme suffering of Sister Leonia's death was very hard to accept. Was Mother Teresa training the sisters as well as she could? Hadn't she cautioned them again and again about dog bites? Try as she might, she could not remember actually saying that to Sister Leonia. Mother Teresa's days were so busy. How could she remember everything?

"I can't do it without You, Lord. Give me strength," she prayed.

Mother Teresa was not invulnerable herself. That same year, riding in a car on a road near Darjeeling, she hit her head when the car stopped suddenly. Nineteen stitches closed the wound.

Alarmed, Indira Gandhi, now India's minister of information, rushed to visit her. Mother Teresa, resting at her own Shishu Bhavan in Darjeeling, recovered well but for a while had to take medicine that made her drowsy. Nevertheless, she would not do less. She would do more. And just as Archbishop Perier allowed Mother Teresa to visit Chota Nagpur before her order was officially allowed to expand outside the diocese, now through the prompting of Archbishop Knox in New Delhi, she visited Venezuela before her order was officially allowed to expand outside of India.

In the fall of 1964, Mother Teresa visited Bishop Benitez in Barquisimeto, Venezuela. Not far from the north coast of Venezuela, the town of about two hundred thousand hugged the foothills of the Cordillera. The mountains were formidable, rising from near sea level to over sixteen thousand feet. Venezuela, even the area around Barquisimeto, was not a poor country. It was riddled with copper mines and oil fields. But, as in America, great wealth did not mean there were no poor people.

"We have thousands of descendants of black slaves brought in decades and decades ago to work the copper mines, Mother," explained the bishop. "They are the poorest of the poor now. Scratching out a living. Many of the women are forced into prostitution. The poor are exploited in every way known to the devil."

Mother Teresa stayed at a boarding school run by Salesian sisters. During the day, Father Tomas and Father Manuel took her to visit a region called the Zona Negro, or Black Belt. The area was lush, tropical lowland. Small family gardens were common. Fields of corn and sugarcane were interspersed with plots of trees bearing mangoes or huge green limes or a kind of cooking banana called plantain. Villages consisted of crude cane-shoot huts sealed with mud and a few more ambitious huts of mud bricks. Paint was rare. So were electricity and tap water. Life was primitive.

"Yet there seems to be food for the people," marveled Mother Teresa.

"Yes, there is food," replied the priests. "As long as they are willing to work the land, they can eke out a living. But if they should stumble, the fall is long and hard."

At one village the priests explained to a few natives who Mother Teresa was and what she did. In no time dozens of bedraggled mothers, clutching half-naked children, surrounded them. Mother Teresa didn't need to know Spanish to know what these desperate mothers were asking. She had seen thousands of such anxious mothers in India. Did the mother have medicine with her now? No? Well then, when were the mother and her sisters coming? Perhaps not at all? Their eyes were crying with need.

At San Felipe, a town of about twenty thousand, the priests showed Mother Teresa a fairly new church. It was their headquarters. From there the two, with a third priest, served about thirty-five villages. Five miles farther on, they entered a small village called Cocorote. It had a small white stucco church with an unused rectory.

"We celebrate Mass here once a week," volunteered one of the priests.

"That unused rectory could be used for a house for the sisters if the bishop is willing," mused Mother Teresa. "And Mass is held once a week, so the sisters will get the spiritual nourishment they need." She looked at the two fathers. "Cocorote seems a promising spot for a house for the sisters."

Mother Teresa returned to India. The church was not frivolous. Even though her order hadn't existed for the usual thirty to fifty years, she suspected an announcement any day that would signal a new era for the Missionaries of Charity!

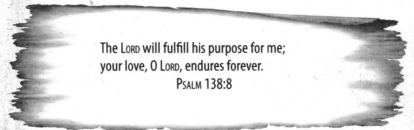

The LORD will fulfill his purpose for me;
your love, O LORD, endures forever.
PSALM 138:8

13

AN ORDER WITHOUT BORDERS

The pope has opened the entire world to the sisters!" gasped one of the clerics in Calcutta.

On February 1, 1965, the Holy See issued the *Decretum Laudis* or Decree of Praise for the Missionaries of Charity. This meant that Cardinal Agaginian of the Sacred Congregation of the Propagation of Faith had finally processed the order's expanded constitution from Mother Teresa and recommendations of the order from various clerics. The pope himself had granted pontifical rights to Mother Teresa's order. The order was now universal rather than being limited to one country.

Mother Teresa could not bring herself to act surprised. "We have much work to do now, Sisters."

She decided to send four sisters to Cocorote in Venezuela as soon as possible. These four would be followed shortly by three more. The first four were all Indian sisters: one from Bengal on the east, another from Nepal to the far north, a third from Mangalore from Karnataka on the southwest coast, and another from Kerala in southernmost India. Mother Teresa's announcement to send four Missionaries of Charity, all Indians, to Venezuela was greeted by Indians with astonished pride.

"Imagine," gushed some, "India sending missionaries to the rest of the world!"

It was decided that their distinctive habits of blue-bordered white saris would be worn even outside India. If it was cold, the nun could add a dark gray cardigan sweater as Mother Teresa often did. If it was even colder, they could add a dark coat. But sweaters and coats were certainly not needed in Cocorote. Mother Teresa accompanied her team to Venezuela. They received a great honor on the way. In Rome, they stopped at the pope's invitation to be blessed.

Pope Paul VI repeated what he had told them in India. "To belong to Christ Jesus is a great gift of God's love. And may the world always see this love in your *smile*!"

At such times Mother Teresa fought the pride she felt for her own efforts. Much prayer was needed to squelch such feelings. Yet, to be approved of by the pope was so very important for her order.

Later, back in Calcutta, Mother Teresa realized how, eighteen years after separation and independence from

Great Britain, certain areas of India were still turbulent. Now that Nehru, the Kashmir Brahmin, was dead, Pakistan challenged more than ever India's claim to the state of Kashmir where many Muslims lived. The region was mountainous, perfect for guerilla warfare. So Pakistani guerrillas constantly harassed Indian troops. Hours after signing a cease-fire agreement, a worn-out President Shastri died of a heart attack. The new prime minister of India was none other than Mother Teresa's personal friend, Indira Gandhi!

"Bless her," said Mother Teresa. "And maybe she can cut some red tape for us."

These sentiments came because international work was much more complicated. There were many money restrictions. For example, no money could be taken out of India. Indira Gandhi would not be able to do anything about that. But perhaps she could speed up supplies moving through customs. Perhaps she could speed up the issuing of passports. How could Mother Teresa keep on top of all this activity? God must continue to help her. And she must remain just as unflappable now as she was many years before when she plopped down in the pharmacist's store and said prayers until he had a change of heart!

In 1966, on the way back from a trip to Venezuela, Mother Teresa stopped in Rome. There she saw Lazar again. He was trying hard to get Mama and Agatha out of Albania. The only response he had from Albanian

MOTHER TERESA ON THE FORGOTTEN:

I can never forget the experience I had in visiting a home where they kept all these old parents of sons and daughters who had just put them into an institution and forgotten them. I saw these old people had everything—good food, comfortable living, television—but everyone was looking toward the door. And I did not see a single one with a smile on his face. I turned to a Sister and I asked, "Why do these people who have every comfort here, why are they all looking toward the door? Why are they not smiling?" And the Sister said: "This is the way it is nearly every day. They are expecting, they are hoping that a son or daughter will come to visit them. They are hurt because they are forgotten."

officials after much effort was that the two women were "unfit to travel." Mama was now eighty-one, with how many years left? Mother Teresa went to the Albanian Embassy herself. There she moved an official to tears with her plea for exit visas for the two women in Tirana. She left hopeful. But over the next months she received no news from officials, although letters could still be exchanged with Mama and Agatha.

It was heartbreaking to read in Agatha's most recent letter Mama's words to Lazar and her little flower bud, Gonxha: "Even if we never meet again in this sad world, we shall surely meet in heaven."

"Oh God," prayed Mother Teresa, "I understand and accept my own sufferings. But it is hard to understand and accept Mama's suffering, when all she wants in her old age is to see me and Lazar again."

In 1967, at the presiding bishop's invitation, Mother Teresa returned to Colombo in Ceylon. Colombo had given Mother Teresa her first taste of the Orient. It was dear to her heart. The looks of the swarming seaport had not changed much in thirty-eight years.

Ceylon was even more complex than India. It had three religions besides Christianity: Hindu, Muslim, and the predominant Buddhism. Many languages were spoken beside the semiofficial Sinhalese: English, Tamil, even Arabic. The Ceylonese had been apprehensive about their independence in 1948. Many wanted Britain to stay, but the English had walked away from Ceylon, just as they'd walked away from India.

Ever since independence, each new governing party of Ceylon had been so unsatisfactory that the voters had thrown it out and replaced it with another. After a while they simply recycled the old parties.

In 1967 the party of Dudley Senanayake reigned. Few Ceylonese thought his well-worn foreign and domestic policies would solve high unemployment and food shortages. Socialist groups were growing and, within them, violent radicals who called themselves the People's Liberation Front. This movement had already torn apart the country of Vietnam.

Mother Teresa was not deterred. "Did I not myself venture from the convent at the moment of India's most violent history? Service to Christ knows nothing about wars." So Mother Teresa established a house in Colombo.

Her next candidate was even more surprising: Rome! Unbelievably, Pope Paul VI himself had asked Mother Teresa to consider placing a house in Rome. This was a great act of humility on his part. And it was so laudatory to Mother Teresa's order that she prayed hard for humility.

"Well, it just means," she told the sisters after much prayer, "that His Holiness wishes our order to join the dozens of other orders already in Rome. It is not because we wretched sisters can solve all the problems of the poor."

Mother Teresa soon saw the problem. Like so many large cities all over the world, Rome had a vast sprawl of shacks growing uncontrollably on its fringes. They had no facilities: no water, no electricity, no sewage disposal, no streetlights. So it was in a shantytown on the southeast fringe of Rome that the sisters began their service. Nearby loomed the red-brown stone of the Aqueduct Felice, one of the "modern" aqueducts of Rome, a mere four hundred years old.

That same year, the sisters also started a house in the African country of Tanzania. The country was a mere four years old, created from Tanganyika and Zanzibar. There were many Catholics in Tanzania. The official languages were English and Swahili, a dialect of the widespread Bantu language.

Over five hundred miles inland from the Indian Ocean was Tabora, a town of about twenty thousand people, between two famous African locales: Lake Tanganyika and the grassy plains of the Serengeti. An old community and crossroads, Tabora displayed both Christian churches and Muslim mosques with their minarets. There Archbishop Mark Mihayo provided the Missionaries of Charity with a compound formerly used by the White Sisters of Africa.

"The compound buildings here are quite old," explained the priest who acted as a guide for Mother Teresa. "Their mud bricks, plastered, are stable in this heat and dryness. But they have suffered during the short but savage rainy seasons. Much repair work is required."

"And when does the rainy season start?" she asked.

He gazed at the sun-bleached sky. "You wouldn't suspect it by the blue sky today, but it will start in a few weeks."

Mother Teresa saw natives gathering out of curiosity across the dirt road from the compound. They carried that vacant, hopeless, unwanted look of the poorest of the poor. "This will be a perfect place to do something beautiful for God," she said.

Within days the natives confirmed her prediction.

Gathering at the compound were the unwanted babies, the orphans, the dying, the unfed, the sick, the lepers, the poorest of the poor. Government officials cautioned her not to use the word *poor*. That was not polite. So to the sisters, the poor became simply "our people," just as Mama had politely called the poor who came to their home in Skopje so many years before.

"And now this," said Mother Teresa to one of the sisters in 1968. "On my way through London, I'm supposed to give an interview on television. To a man named Muggery, I think."

How she disliked interviews. Still, she was obedient. And could she turn down an interview if she influenced just one person to serve Christ because of it? No, it was unthinkable. The interview for the British Broadcasting Company (the BBC) was to take place at the Holy Child Convent in Cavendish Square. Mother Teresa was late. She was introduced to the waiting television crew.

"And this is your host, Malcolm Muggeridge," someone said, gesturing to a florid, impish-faced man with intense watery eyes.

"Bless you, Mr. Muggeridge," she said, giving the Indian gesture of respect, palms held together.

"I lived in Calcutta for a while," he said sharply, returning the gesture impatiently. "This way. Come along, Mother Teresa!"

He escorted her to a room where the cameras had been set up. Muggeridge was well prepared. His questions were curt and to the point. Mother Teresa was nervous, her answers halting and short, completely uncontroversial. Muggeridge looked disappointed, then uneasy, as if they might not have enough material for a half-hour program.

"Don't you think what you and your sisters are trying to do could be better handled by a government agency?" he probed.

"The more help to the poor, the better," she replied. "But we offer love."

Muggeridge blinked. "Well, in view of the commonly held opinion that there are too many people in India, why save a few babies that were destined to die?"

Now Mother Teresa blinked. Did God put too many stars in the sky? "I will never turn away a baby. Our way is to preserve life, the life of Christ in the life of the child." *There can never be enough children,* she thought to herself. *Children are the life of God.*

After the interview, Mr. Muggeridge looked disappointed. Mother Teresa heard mutterings about how the interview might have to be shown very late at night. The lighting was poor, not to mention the fact that the interview was devoid of confrontation. Mother Teresa hadn't even asked for money. Some on the television crew acted as if they would be just as happy if the interview was never shown at all.

Mother Teresa shrugged the event off. What was to happen with the interview was God's business. Her task was simply to be obedient.

MOTHER TERESA ON WESTERN POVERTY:

I found the poverty of the West so much more difficult to remove. When I pick up a person from the street, hungry, I give him a plate of rice, a piece of bread, and he is satisfied. I have removed that hunger. But a person that is shut out, that feels unwanted, unloved, terrified, the person that has been thrown out from society—that poverty hurts so much, and I find that very difficult.

The next year, Mother Teresa opened a house in Bourke, Australia. Bourke was a small town of three thousand people located in southwestern Australia beside the Darling River. In this bleak, sparsely populated scrubland, the poorest of the poor were aborigines. The invitation had come from an old friend: James Knox, now a cardinal in Australia.

"The 'abos' are caught between two cultures, in a no-man's-land, much like Native Americans," explained an Australian.

Mother Teresa appreciated the fact that the local did not judge the aborigines, but simply stated a stark truth. She was not a social worker. She provided free services to the poorest of the poor. With it came love.

That same year Mother Teresa realized another of her dreams. She had wanted a lay society dedicated to the same goals as the orders of the sisters and brothers. This was not without precedent. There had been such orders among the Franciscans and Benedictines. But Mother Teresa envisioned her order cutting across religious differences. One would not have to be Catholic or even Christian to be a "coworker." Coworkers were to be united in a common goal of "wholehearted service to the poorest of the poor."

This lay society would be loosely organized, operating in the most frugal manner possible. The firm grounding of their spirituality would, of course, be in prayer. Mother Teresa had always believed prayer led to faith, faith to love, love to service. She would urge any layperson to pray daily with the sisters and brothers the famous prayer of Saint Francis of Assisi:

> Lord, make me an instrument of your peace,
> That where there is hatred, I may bring love;
> That where there is wrong,
> I may bring the spirit of forgiveness,
> That where there is discord, I may bring harmony;
> That where there is error, I may bring truth;
> That where there is doubt, I may bring faith;
> That where there is despair, I may bring hope;
> That where there are shadows, I may bring light;
> That where there is sadness, I may bring joy.

Lord, grant that I may seek rather to comfort, than to
*   be comforted;*
To understand than to be understood;
To love than be loved,
For it is by forgetting self that one finds;
It is by dying that one awakens to eternal life.

In Rome, Mother Teresa told Pope Paul VI her
dream. "Go ahead," he said, "I'll be your first coworker."
Thrilled, she met with her longtime, very loyal friend,
Ann Blaikie, and several others. The wife of an English
businessman in Calcutta and an active Catholic, Ann
Blaikie had visited Kalighat in 1954. She had been in-
flamed by the love practiced by the Missionaries of Charity. In one way or another, she had been involved with
Mother Teresa ever since, even after she and her family
went back to London in 1960. She never forgot how
Mother Teresa offered service to all the poor.

Together again in Rome, the two women drafted the
constitution of the International Association of Coworkers of Mother Teresa. Three days later the new constitution was presented to Pope Paul VI himself. He gave
it his blessing. It was astonishing how Mother Teresa
now had access to power. Cardinal Agaginian issued his
Decree of Praise, and the coworkers, united in prayer and
sacrifice, began their good works and free service to the
poorest of the poor of all castes and creeds.

Mother Teresa urged her coworkers to pray a second

prayer every day as well as the prayer of Saint Francis, just as the sisters and brothers did. It was from Pope Paul VI:

> *Make us worthy, Lord,*
> *To serve our fellowmen*
> *Throughout the world*
> *Who live and die in poverty and hunger.*
> *Give them, through our hands,*
> *This day their daily bread;*
> *And by our understanding love,*
> *Give peace and joy.*

Ann Blaikie was the first chair of the coworkers. The coworkers helped in any way they could. Their goals were those of Mother Teresa. Needs of the houses of the Missionaries of Charity and the Missionary Brothers of Charity were extensive and soon well-known to the coworkers: medicines, vitamins, trays, syringes, needles, bandages, condensed milk, canned baby foods, clothing, bedding, rags, sandals, blankets. Many coworkers labored only at collecting these supplies and sending them to the various houses. This effort in itself was a great service. And Mother Teresa made it clear she did not want them raising funds. Material help, yes. Money, no.

"Somehow the money comes anyway," she said. "And I don't want our organizations to become known for asking for money."

She had to reeducate some well-intentioned helpers.

No coworker was to be paid. No offices were to be maintained. Slick newsletters were anathema to her. Collecting centers were never to be in rented space, but rather in donated space in garages, churches, and private homes. No help was too small.

"Many people want to do big things," she explained. "No one wants to do the small things—writing a letter for a blind man, washing someone's dirty clothes, cleaning someone's tiny house."

The end of the decade saw a growing force doing small things for the poorest of the poor under Mother Teresa. The core of her organization was her Missionaries of Charity. There were now 585 sisters. Candidates applied at the rate of 100 per year. They came from more than a dozen countries.

By the end of 1969, the Missionaries of Charity had founded twenty-five houses all over India and five in other countries. But this did not begin to tell the whole story. For example, the house at Calcutta ran sixty different enterprises! The House of the Dying in Calcutta alone had taken in over twenty thousand of the most destitute. Half they saved. The tiny school in Moti Jihl that once had only five children now had five hundred.

In a similar way, each of the thirty houses or foundations of the Missionaries of Charity ran numerous enterprises that served orphans, the dying, the sick, lepers, the unfed, and the poor, uneducated children.

Then there were Mother Teresa's complementary

groups: the Missionary Brothers of Charity and the coworkers. The brothers numbered nearly one hundred. The coworkers, although loosely organized, had all the appearances of growing at a phenomenal rate. Embryonic organizations seemed to be born in country after country, each chaired by Ann Blaikie and a cochair from that country.

John Southworth, who had introduced Mother Teresa to Malcolm Muggeridge the previous year, was cochair of the coworkers in England. Would thousands upon thousands of coworkers arise? If so, would they be disciplined enough to give wholehearted free service to the poorest of the poor?

In London, Mother Teresa was told a BBC executive had insisted her interview with Malcolm Muggeridge be shown Sunday evening and not late at night as some of the disappointed television crew had suggested. She had forgotten about the program. The program was received like no other in Muggeridge's career, she was told. The program had to be repeated. She had not asked for money, but money poured into the BBC, the equivalent of over fifty thousand dollars. Mother Teresa had reached their heart as no one else before. The money was turned over to her coworkers in London. Of course, BBC wanted another interview.

"And, I say, what about letting us film you at your work for a one-hour television program?" they enthused. "In jolly old Calcutta?"

She knew the work of the brothers and sisters could use good publicity, but there was now a fawning attitude toward her she didn't like. People were treating her like a celebrity. It was wrong. And how could she spare the time?

"No," she said.

> "If my people, who are called by my name, will humble themselves and pray and seek my face and turn from their wicked ways, then will I hear from heaven and will forgive their sin and will heal their land."
>
> 2 CHRONICLES 7:14

14

SOMETHING BEAUTIFUL FOR GOD

The BBC reacted to Mother Teresa's refusal by going over her head. Soon a letter arrived from Cardinal Heenen of London. "Couldn't Mother Teresa let the world know of her good work for the poorest of the poor?" he asked.

Before she could reply to the cardinal, her archbishop of Calcutta also suggested she let the world understand her work. Didn't she know there was a hunger in people to help? And wasn't that a way to maybe find faith?

So she wrote to the BBC: "If this TV programme is going to help people to love God better, then we will have it, but with one condition—that the brothers and sisters be included, as they do the work."[1]

She gave the television crew five days. They arrived in early 1969, quickly wearing the beleaguered look of newcomers to Calcutta's heat and humidity. It was not even the rainy season yet. None of the crew complained of having only five days as Mother Teresa received them in the courtyard of the motherhouse.

They glanced into her tiny office. They were stunned to learn it was the nerve center of her huge operation. She had one typewriter. She had finally relented and allowed a telephone. As often as not, she answered it herself: "Mother Teresa speaking."

"There is a general strike in Calcutta," she told the television crew, "but it shouldn't slow you down."

She was amused by the crew. She knew that Malcolm Muggeridge, who shot back clever retorts faster than anyone she had ever known, was the celebrated face that showed up on the television screen. But his director, Peter Chafer, was in charge. He bossed Muggeridge around. Muggeridge seemed more and more subdued anyway, as if awed by the simple life of the sisters. The cameraman and soundman began setting up equipment in the courtyard.

"Come now and meet the Master of the house," she told the others, leading them to the chapel. "With Christ, we can do anything. Without Christ, we can do nothing," she explained. "If we didn't take every day the Holy Sacrament—what you call Holy Communion—we would be helpless."

As they returned to the courtyard, she told them they were all welcome to attend Mass with her and the sisters in the morning. She would save a space for them and provide them with a missal. She was pleased that Malcolm Muggeridge showed up every morning as Brother Andrew celebrated the Mass. The general strike made services easier for outsiders, too. The usual traffic noise coming in the windows that faced Lower Circular Road was muted. Mother Teresa noticed that Malcolm Muggeridge didn't take part in the Holy Sacrament but seemed deeply affected by it.

At the House of the Dying, the small miracle happened to this crew from BBC that happened all the time to visitors. First of all they were horrified at the sight of the emaciated dying, almost paralyzed by the doom. Then they gushed pity for the poor unwanted creatures. Then from personal contact with the battered, the elderly, and the diseased, the visitors came to realize that the pitiful creatures were real people, endearing and lovable. Love pushed aside all lesser thoughts. How could one not give comfort to these dear personal friends?

But the film crew knew filming inside Nirmal Hriday

was virtually impossible. "The light is too poor to film," insisted the cameraman. "We brought only one floodlight. It simply isn't enough in this dimly lit House of the Dying."

They filmed anyway. To make sure they came away with something they could use, they filmed patients sitting in the sunshine in the courtyard. They went on to film the children at Shishu Bhavan. They filmed the schools, the lepers. Sometimes Muggeridge was completely overcome. He stumbled off camera, tears streaming down his face. When he learned the lepers were making money by printing pamphlets on a printing press purchased by Mother Teresa, he was confounded.

"But what do you know of printing presses? How do you have time to. . ." The questions died in his throat.

The crew finished their filming, certain that much of the film was useless. Often the cans of sensitive film sat baking in the scorching Calcutta sun. And there were the lighting problems in dim interiors. Mother Teresa was only sorry that the crew felt badly about it. God would decide if the film was part of His plan or not.

She thought about Malcolm Muggeridge after the crew left. She was sure he had at last seen the suffering Jesus in the faces of her poor. Yes, in spite of his caustic wit, he was a very receptive man. He had crumpled under the face of Jesus. He seemed without a church. He seemed removed from the Holy Communion. That bothered her very much, because she knew his heart was ready for the real Jesus.

She had to write him a letter:

Very often in my heart a desire has come to be in England when you make your first Holy Communion with Jesus. I don't know—but Jesus never gives desires which He does not mean to fulfill.[2]

Muggeridge wrote back that the film, much of which they had been ready to scrap, turned out beautifully—especially in the House of the Dying. The crew was stunned. There was no logic to it. It simply could not have happened. It was as if love illuminated the place. Muggeridge carried on so much about it publicly that he angered skeptics. There had to be a technical explanation, they insisted. But Muggeridge knew the only explanation was a miracle: love illuminated the interior of the House of the Dying!

Then he explained to Mother Teresa why he could not join a church or participate in the Holy Sacrament. In England he saw politics and hypocrisy all too often in the church.

She wrote back:

I believe the film has brought people closer to God, and so your and my hope has been fulfilled. I think now more than ever that you should use the beautiful gift God has given you for His greater glory. All that you can be and do—let it all be for Him and

*Him alone. Today what is happening in the surface
of the Church will pass. For Christ, the Church is the
same, today, yesterday, and tomorrow. The Apostles
went through the same feeling of fear and distrust,
failure and disloyalty, and yet Christ did not scold
them. Just: "Little children, little faith—why did you
fear?"*[3]

Did she detect Muggeridge's resistance weakening? She wrote him again. Likening him to Nicodemus, the wise elder who longed to believe Jesus but struggled with doubts, she insisted Muggeridge must "receive the kingdom of God as a little child." He must put aside his worldly concerns. Only then would he understand why his longing for God was so intense. Only then would he feel the infinite love Christ had for him personally.

The television program, released in early 1970, was well received. Mother Teresa heard all the details from Muggeridge himself in December of that year when she went to London to open another house of the Missionaries of Charity. The house was in the area called Southall, which was known for its Indian immigrants. It was not only a house but also a novitiate for training novices from Europe and the Americas. So many women wanted to serve in her worldwide organization for the poorest of the poor that they could not all be trained at the motherhouse in Calcutta. With Mother Teresa traveling more and more, the training of sisters in the right way was never more important. But she had always known that.

Was Mother Teresa surprised when Cardinal Heenen came to celebrate the first Mass in the house in Southall? "If Jesus can come, surely the cardinal can come also," she noted.

She learned Muggeridge had transformed his Calcutta experience into a book titled *Something Beautiful for God*, after one of her favorite expressions. He also included many of her favorite prayers and thoughts on silence and other things she had written out for him on nine pages. All royalties were to be directed to the Mother Teresa Committee. It would be published in April 1970.

Meanwhile Mother Teresa received distressing news from her sister in Albania. Agatha wrote that Mama was fading. At eighty-five years of age, Mama weighed less than ninety pounds. Mother Teresa planned a trip to Yugoslavia. Who knew what she might be able to do from there?

But before she was able to leave, Mother Teresa was called to Rome. On January 6, 1970, Pope Paul VI presented her with the Pope John XXIII Peace Prize. This prize had been set up by the late pope to honor the peacemakers who answered his appeal for peace in his encyclical *Pacem in Terris*.

Once again Mother Teresa felt too visible, too honored, this time in a sea of cardinals and bishops. And the pope himself, so much more the servant of Christ than she, praised her. But what could she do? The prize was

MOTHER TERESA ON UNWANTED CHILDREN:

And this I appeal in India, I appeal everywhere: Let us bring the child back, and this year being the child's year: What have we done for the child? At the beginning of the year I told, I spoke everywhere and I said: Let us make this the year that we make every single child born, and unborn, wanted.

really from two great popes. And it carried twenty-five thousand dollars with it. Could she deny that money to the poorest of the poor because she wanted to indulge her humility? Dare she even dwell on her own wants?

"I accept whatever God gives me," she prayed.

In April of that year, just a few days before Mother Teresa was to leave with five sisters to open a second house in Australia, she fell and broke her arm. She was not surprised. It seemed that before she realized some wonderful dream, she often had to suffer first. She had the head injury just before she went to Venezuela. She accepted it with joy. Suffering only brought her closer to Jesus.

This time, the doctor told her she should not travel to Australia. She insisted. To protect her from her "foolishness," the doctor bound her arm and secured it to her body. She left, feeling like she was in a body cast.

By the time she and the sisters reached Melbourne, where they planned a house to serve derelicts, Mother Teresa was fed up with being a mummy. The sisters removed much of the binding. The provincial of the Loreto nuns in Melbourne helped them find a house. It was badly neglected and had a leaking roof and a filthy floor.

Just as she had always done, Mother Teresa started cleaning right away, this time with one arm. That was why she could ask so much of her sisters: because she always gave so much herself. That night the sisters stacked their only blankets on one side of Mother Teresa's cot so she could rest her broken arm. The next morning the sisters found themselves covered with the blankets.

"It gets cold in the night here in late April," commented Mother Teresa. "The Australian winter is coming."

In June she flew to Belgrade, Yugoslavia, then worked her way south toward Skopje where the bishop had encouraged her to open a house sometime in the future. She remembered how Mama thought she would never travel because of her vow of poverty. Now she traveled constantly, although she could not travel to the one place she wanted to visit most: Albania.

Once again Mother Teresa saw Prizren, the hometown of her mother and father. It was a town now of about fifty thousand, yet it still featured clustered stucco and stone buildings topped by red tile. Muslim-inspired domes seemed everywhere, with a few stiletto-like minarets poking into the sky. It was much like she remembered it. Had the 1963 earthquake not affected Prizren?

In Skopje, which she remembered so much better, she saw the damage all too well. Yes, the old Roman bridge across the Vardar was there, as were most other famous landmarks, including the famous caravansary. But many old buildings were gone, including the old train station with its tender memories. Only the old station clock remained, as a monument frozen at the exact moment of the first earth-quake tremor: 5:17. Her old Church of the Sacred Heart on Vlaska Street was gone. Her home was gone, too. And in the cemetery there wasn't a trace of Papa's grave!

"We must go up Black Mountain," she insisted with some dread.

Nothing on earth is forever, she reminded herself. There was no horse-drawn coach this time. A car sputtered up the mountainside. Praise God! There once again loomed the large single cupola so typical of the monasteries around Skopje. Inside the building, Mother Teresa knelt to pray. She had spent many hours of uncertainty in this place back in 1927 and 1928. And how perfectly her life had turned out.

Afterward, reflecting on the statue of Mary, her blessed Madonna of Cernagore at Letnica, Mother Teresa quipped to her companions, "At least *her* face is still the same after forty-two years."

A crisis in India drew Mother Teresa back to Calcutta in the spring of 1971. The province of Bengal, poor as

MOTHER TERESA ON JOY:

Let us keep that joy of loving Jesus in our hearts. And share that joy with all that we come in touch with. And that radiating joy is real, for we have no reason not to be happy because we have Christ with us. Christ in our hearts, Christ in the poor that we meet, Christ in the smile that we give and the smile that we receive.

it was, was once again the victim of outside influences. West Pakistan was fighting East Pakistan, just east of Bengal. East Pakistan had declared its independence as the new country of Bangladesh. Caught in the middle were Hindu Pakistanis, who came flooding into Bengal. Ten million of them!

Hundreds of thousands of them sought refuge in Calcutta, the poorest of cities. They took shelter in giant sewer pipes stored for use in a new development. Mother Teresa knew the refugees not only had to be fed, but protected against disease, as well. Cholera, smallpox, and dysentery would soon run wild in such a setting. The Missionaries of Charity, indeed it seemed all of India, rushed help to the refugees.

"India has been wonderful in accepting and taking care of the millions of Pakistan refugees, and we in India will take care of them," said Mother Teresa publicly. "In opening the door to them, the Indian prime minister, Mrs. Gandhi, has done a wonderful, Christlike thing."

Later, she heard that Malcolm Muggeridge at the ceremony in London for the release of his *Something Beautiful for God* book was talking about Mother Teresa winning some award called the Nobel Prize. How she disliked such talk. But could she refuse any award if it added one rupee to the poorest of the poor?

All through 1970 and 1971, the Missionaries of Charity had been adding houses in India as well as more international houses: one more in London, one more in Australia, two more in Venezuela, the first one in Jordan, and the first in the United States!

In the fall of 1971, Mother Teresa went to New York to publicize the release of the American version of Muggeridge's *Something Beautiful for God*, but she had something else in mind, too. Cardinal Cooke had invited the order to the archdiocese of New York City. South Bronx with its Hispanic immigrants drew her. The root of their squalor and hopelessness was not the same as Calcutta's. Many of these poor were brought down by drugs. Could Mother Teresa and her sisters deal with this new problem? Only time would tell.

On October 18, 1971, Mother Teresa opened the new house in the South Bronx. As usual the vow of poverty was strictly obeyed. Mother Teresa arrived with but five sisters, carrying only their bedrolls. The house had six old metal beds with springs, one table, two benches, a cupboard, and bookshelves. A supply of old wooden boxes of various sizes would serve for the rest of the furniture.

"God provides," commented the sisters cheerily.

Not every endeavor was successful. On August 25, 1971, the Missionaries of Charity were dealt their first major setback: Ceylon. Dudley Senanayake had failed in the eyes of the populace. Socialists had swept him out of office in 1970. The Socialists began fighting with an even more radical group, the Communists. Civil war had broken out in March 1971 and raged week after week.

The sisters were told by the government to leave. They were told it was for their own safety, but Mother Teresa suspected that the sisters confronting head-on the social ills of a miserably governed Ceylon was an embarrassment to the Socialists. The People's Liberation Front ranted constantly about their presence. The rebels were put down after six months, but the sisters were gone. So was Ceylon. It was now a hard-line Socialist country called Sri Lanka.

"Failure is nothing but the kiss of Jesus," said Mother Teresa with complete conviction.

> "I am the vine; you are the branches. If a man remains in me and I in him, he will bear much fruit; apart from me you can do nothing."
>
> John 15:5

15

THE MISSION CONTINUES

Missionaries of Charity houses continued to multiply: two in Bangladesh, another in Australia, one in the troubled enclave of Gaza in Israel, one in Yemen, one in Ethiopia. Once again the sisters tasted failure. The house in Belfast was short-lived, hurriedly closed by church officials who seemed to know about some terrible threat to the sisters.

Then Mother Teresa was hit by a personal loss. In July of 1972, Mama passed away. The pain of her loss was bearable only when Mother Teresa recalled Mama's words: "We shall surely meet in heaven." Of course Mother Teresa believed that with all her heart and soul.

Just two years later, Agatha also passed away, at only sixty-eight years of age. "Did she, the ever-faithful caretaker, her duty done, just pine away?" asked Mother Teresa.

Awards continued to come. Prince Philip of Britain presented the Templeton Prize for Progress in Religion to her in 1973. With it came a very large sum of money from Mr. Templeton, a financial tycoon. Mother Teresa, in accepting the award money, said:

We thank God that [Mr. Templeton] *had the courage to give, to be spent for the glory of God, the fund that he received so generously from God. In giving this award to me, actually it is given to the people, to all those who share with me throughout the world in the work of love, in spreading God's love amongst men.*

Actually we are touching His body. It is the hunger of Christ that we are feeding, it is the naked Christ that we are clothing, it is the homeless Christ that we are giving shelter and it is not just hunger for bread, and nakedness for cloth, and homelessness for a house made of bricks but Christ today is hungry in our poor people, and even in the rich, for love, for being cared for, for being wanted, for having someone to call their own.

Today, like before, when Jesus comes amongst His own, his own don't know Him. He comes in the rotten bodies of our poor, He comes even in the rich, who are being suffocated with their riches, in the loneliness of their hearts, and there is no one to love them. And here Jesus comes to you and to me.[1]

The Missionaries of Charity benefited from more than award money. In 1975 the Imperial Chemical Industries turned over to them its great compound in Tiljala. It would become an all-purpose compound that sheltered volunteers from overseas, the mentally disabled, vocational courses for the poor, and small cottage industries. The complex became known as *Prem Dan*, or Gift of Love.

In late 1975, Mother Teresa saw her own sixty-five-year-old, weather-beaten face displayed on the cover of *Time* magazine. A large caption read "Living Saints." The story inside lauded her. The international magazine increased her renown, something she cared nothing for. In fact, she dreaded it. Becoming a celebrity was the antithesis of all her vows. But there was always that justification of fame that she could not deny: as an object of curiosity, she publicized the need for more help for the poorest of the poor.

By 1975, with over one hundred houses and over one thousand sisters to direct, Mother Teresa could no longer keep up her close personal knowledge of all the sisters. Who could? When Father Le Joly asked her just how well she still knew her sisters, he was not being critical.

"I no longer know every novice and postulant," she admitted with regret. "There are over three hundred now."

Father Le Joly smiled. "Are you saying that you still know all seven hundred of the professed sisters?"

"Yes. I know each one personally."

And she did. She knew each one, where she served and her strong and weak points. Did one have a special gift for training? Mother knew. Did one have a talent for medicine? Mother knew. Was one too strict to handle sensitive young postulants? Mother knew. She had always considered training the sisters the most important function she had, in spite of opening new houses. After all, the order must continue beyond her time on earth. That would happen only if she trained the sisters the right way.

She was obedient, and she expected obedience. Once a reporter asked if the sisters taking their final vows asked to be assigned to certain houses. Mother Teresa replied, "They go where they are sent." She didn't elaborate, but she could have told many stories of when she'd asked a sister to go to a certain house in India and she fully expected her to be on the evening train. "After all, they own almost nothing," she reasoned. "Any sister can pack her bedroll and bucket in ten minutes."

In 1976 Mother Teresa founded the contemplative branch of the Missionaries of Charity in a convent in the Bronx. This was another of her dreams. There the sisters spent almost their entire day in prayer. They were similar to contemplatives of the Carmelites, but the Missionaries of Charity were not cloistered. For two hours a day, the sisters would go out to visit the sick or the imprisoned. They counseled about God to any crying spirit who came to them: the drunkard, the drug addict, the lonely, the aged. They were to serve the spiritually poorest of

MOTHER TERESA ON DRUG USE:

I was surprised in the West to see so many young boys and girls given into drugs, and I tried to find out why—why is it like that, and the answer was: Because there is no one in the family to receive them. Father and mother are so busy they have no time. Young parents are in some institution and the child takes back to the street and gets involved in something.

the poor. Mother Teresa picked the very capable Sister Nirmala to lead them.

Soon Mother Teresa planned to start a similar group of contemplatives for men in Rome. That would make five branches. "We will soon tend the five wounds of Jesus with our five branches," she said, as always visualizing Jesus in the suffering.

In October 1975, a series of Silver Jubilees began. Of all the honors Mother Teresa endured, these were the dearest because they really honored the work of the Missionaries of Charity. The first to be honored with the twenty-fifth anniversary was her order, founded in 1950. Just before the Jubilee, Mother Teresa suffered her worst cold since childhood. Surely, once again it was suffering required for such special favors from God.

But Mother Teresa left her sickbed. The sisters celebrated for one week. Every day they went to a different temple or church or synagogue or mosque. They prayed with Jews, Muslims, Sikhs, Protestants, Buddhists, and Hindus. Mother Teresa wanted all hearts united to the one true God in thanksgiving. And of course it was her way to thank everyone who had helped the sisters.

Mary's words from the book of Luke, her Magnificat, caught the spirit of the sisters' thanksgiving exactly:

> *And Mary said, "My soul doth magnify the Lord,*
> *and my spirit hath rejoiced in God my Saviour. . . .*
> *For he that is mighty hath done to me great things;*
> *and holy is his name. And his mercy is on them that*
> *fear him from generation to generation.* (1:46–50 KJV)

The special Mass at the motherhouse was concelebrated by Archbishop Picachy and twenty priests. The chapel was full of joyous people. For this one time there was a pew in the chapel for government officials and other guests. Mother Teresa and all the sisters, including sisters who had come to represent their sisters serving on five other continents, sat on mats. On that very day there were 1,133 sisters worldwide.

The next day Mother Teresa traveled to the old motherhouse at Creek Lane, wearily lugging a picture of Mary up the stairs to the old chapel. And of course she thanked the Gomes family who had been so giving in

MOTHER TERESA ON CHRIST'S SACRIFICE:

Jesus died on the cross because that is what it took for Him to. . .save us from our selfishness in sin. He gave up everything to do the Father's will—to show us that we, too, must be willing to give up everything to do God's will—to love one another as He loves each of us. If we are not willing to give whatever it takes to do good to one another, sin is still in us.

the early years of the order.

"How generously you have served our precious Lord," she said.

Over the next years, Silver Jubilee would follow Silver Jubilee. Just before the anniversary celebration for the House of the Dying, Mother Teresa was leveled by the flu. She suffered gratefully.

Because the new Cardinal Picachy was in Rome, the *pro nuncio* Archbishop Storero celebrated the Mass. There also was Linus Gomes, due to be their new archbishop. After the Mass something miraculous happened. A Hindu priest from the Temple of Kali approached Mother Teresa, bowing in respect with his hands folded.

He cried, "For thirty years I have worshipped the goddess Kali in stone. Today the goddess Mother stands before me."

Of course such exalted reverence embarrassed Mother Teresa. But the man's reverence, misguided though it was, reflected how deeply respected the sisters now were.

"Not our glory, but God's," insisted Mother Teresa repeatedly.

On August 6, 1978, Pope Paul VI died after fifteen years as head of the Roman Catholic Church. Mother Teresa mourned him. He had certainly blessed and shepherded her order. He had suffered much heartache because of the great changes brought by the Second Vatican Council. Many religious opposed the changes. Many religious had left the church. The pope had been in physical pain, too. Although he had to have help walking up stairs, he always went to his knees in Mass. Once someone asked if he suffered excruciating pain doing that. Excruciating was the right word.

"He answered, 'I just live my Mass,'" said Mother Teresa in admiration.

The new pope, formerly Cardinal Luciani of Venice, took the name John Paul I, to honor the preceding two popes. He was a pastoral figure, not a veteran of the Vatican. But Catholics hardly had time to reflect on this pope before he died, after only thirty-four days as pope.

Within days, Cardinal Wojtyla of Poland was elected pope. Mother Teresa knew nothing about him except that at fifty-eight he was young for a pope and he was the first non-Italian pope in 455 years!

"Apparently he is quite poetic," ventured one of the

sisters, who had been talking to the Jesuit priests. "He has published poetry, even a play."

"God speaks through the pope," was all Mother Teresa had to say.

The Missionaries of Charity opened fourteen more international houses in 1979. Mother Teresa seemed to be traveling all the time. She knew people all over the world now. And with that familiarity came pain. In New York she visited Archbishop Fulton Sheen in the hospital. He was eighty-four years old.

"You must not make him talk," warned the nurse.

So it is that bad, she thought sadly. His appearance confirmed it. The most congenial of men, he couldn't muster a smile. He was very close to meeting Jesus. She handed him the tiny statue of Mary that she always carried.

"You have done much for Jesus," she said, and left as he lifted the statue to his lips and kissed it.

By the end of the year, the Missionaries of Charity had 158 houses, of which 86 were in India. Of the 1,718 sisters, 1,187 were professed. They kept statistics, although numbers were repugnant to Mother Teresa. Christ's love was measureless. Still, people wanted to know. In 1979 they assisted 7,632 dying and destitute, most of whom now lived. They ran 495 mobile clinics that provided medical services to a staggering 4.1 million patients. In addition, they treated 258,000 lepers in 103 leprosariums. They ran 107 slum schools with 15,800 students. They provided day care for 900 children. They cared for 2,770 orphans. They regularly fed 165,000 of the poor. They also visited prisons, taught catechism and Sunday school classes, and ran vocational classes—besides counseling on marriage and natural family planning.

And those were just the numbers for the sisters.

The Missionary Brothers of Charity numbered 204, of whom 103 were professed. In 1979 they assisted 320 dying and destitute. They ran 26 mobile clinics that provided medical services to 17,000 patients. In two leprosariums they treated 10,000 lepers. They ran 35 slum schools with 4,442 students. They provided day care for 900 children. They cared for 170 orphans and 180 physically or mentally disabled children. Besides the brothers, there were now nearly 2,000 coworkers in two dozen countries. Their effort was no small contribution to providing wholehearted free service to the poorest of the poor.

But the entire world was to know of Mother Teresa that same year for something else.

> If there is a poor man among your brothers in any of the towns of the land that the LORD your God is giving you, do not be hardhearted or tightfisted toward your poor brother.
>
> DEUTERONOMY 15:7

16

THE NOBEL PRIZE

One day in 1979 when Mother Teresa came back to the motherhouse, the little parlor was choked with reporters.

"I thought I gave strict orders that no reporters were to be allowed in like this," she admonished the sister in the tiny office.

"You have won the Nobel Prize!" the reporters all clamored.

From that moment on there was no letup in telegrams, telephone calls, and letters. The headlines in the Calcutta *Statesman* screamed: JOY SWEPT CALCUTTA.

Mother Teresa could get nothing done. Praise God, it was her time to go on a retreat. For nine days she had peace. She remembered how she had joked about the Nobel Prize with her lepers. She had been rumored a winner for the last several years. With the prize came a

very large sum of money. She had planned with her lepers
exactly how each dollar would be spent building houses
for them.

"So, it's up to you," she had told her lepers, "to pray
and see that it happens."

And so it happened. Mother Teresa traveled to Nor-
way with her first two postulants, Sister Agnes and Sister
Gertrude. She was deluged in Oslo by reporters snapping
flashbulbs in her face and yelling questions. "For enduring
this alone I should go to heaven," she told the sisters in
Bengali.

In her acceptance speech in a somber hall at the Uni-
versity of Oslo, Mother Teresa spoke without notes as always. First, she asked all present to join her in the prayer
of Saint Francis. Then among other heartfelt comments,
she scorched the crime she felt was the most insidious
enemy of peace in the world:

I feel the greatest destroyer of peace today is abortion,

because it is direct war, a direct killing, direct murder by the mother herself. And we read in the scripture, for God says very clearly, "Even if a mother could forget her child, I will not forget you.". . .And that is what strikes me most, the beginning of that sentence, that even if a mother could forget, something impossible. . .

[So] this is what is the greatest destroyer of peace today. Because if a mother can kill her own child, what is left for me to kill you and you to kill me? There is nothing between.

Her fiery message delivered, she finished with humor:

[Some]one asked me, "Are you married?"

And I said, "Yes, and I find it sometimes very difficult to smile at Jesus because He can be so demanding sometimes." This is really true. And there is where the love comes—when it is demanding, and yet we can give it to Him with joy.[1]

Mother Teresa and her lepers had already planned how the $190,000 of prize money would be spent. But to her amazement, she received another award called the People's Prize, money raised for the winner by private citizens in Norway. This year the amount was nearly the same as the Nobel Prize money!

When she learned a sumptuous banquet was planned

after the award ceremonies, Mother Teresa insisted it be canceled and the money spent on the poor. It was replaced by an austere reception at which she drank water.

In Rome on December 13, 1979, Mother Teresa and forty of her sisters were in Pope John Paul II's private chapel. The pope celebrated Mass, then spoke to them in the hall, encouraging them to continue their good work.

"He is as humble and simple as a child," said Mother Teresa on her return to India, enormously pleased. "And he kissed my head right here," she added, pointing to the habit covering the top of her head.

India honored Mother Teresa again. In the presidential palace in Delhi, President Reddy presented her India's highest civilian award: the *Bharat Ratna*, or Jewel of India. He praised her for not just talking about imperatives but doing them. Indira Gandhi came up to congratulate her, too. She was no longer prime minister, voted out after being tainted by a campaign violation. Mother Teresa had paid her a personal visit after her defeat to console her. The two disagreed on many things but remained close friends.

Showing once again she lived the imperatives, Mother Teresa persuaded the government officials to take the dinner they had prepared for a banquet to her House of the Dying in Delhi. There she and the officials fed the destitute by hand.

In 1980, Mother Teresa opened her house in Skopje. The sisters were two Indians, a Maltese, and an Albanian.

"Skopje gave up one sister and now gets four," she quipped. In 1981, Lazar died at age seventy-four, a peaceful death but sad for Mother Teresa. She seemed to be experiencing a series of emotional highs and lows. Her work had never flourished more, yet family and friends were getting old and dying off.

Her faith steadied her. After all, now her entire family was united once again in heaven, just waiting for her. So she began in every meeting with sisters, brothers, and coworkers to warn them to follow their constitutions to the letter. She wouldn't always be with them.

In 1982, God answered another of her prayers. Malcolm Muggeridge, after giving a thousand reasons why he could never join a church, was received into the Catholic Church in England. It was just as she had written him many years earlier: very often in her heart sprang a desire for Muggeridge to make his first Holy Communion with Jesus, and Jesus never gives desires which he does not mean to fulfill. Muggeridge still lauded Mother Teresa at every opportunity, saying his book *Something Beautiful for God* overshadowed all his other accomplishments a millions times over.

That same year she visited her house in Beirut, Lebanon, which was torn apart by civil war. Two factions bitterly fought each other across a no-man's-land called the "green line." Mother Teresa's house was in East Beirut. She soon learned that thirty-seven Muslim children were stranded in an asylum on the other side of the green line in West Beirut. They included the mentally and physically disabled and even the paralyzed. The poor innocents were helpless. They would soon starve.

In spite of protests that snipers were everywhere, not to mention that bombs were falling, Mother Teresa got volunteers to drive vans across the green line. Within hours they had the children back in their house. Mother Teresa busied herself rounding up bedding, food, and supplies.

One Red Cross worker said, "We didn't expect a saint to be so efficient."

She felt like she could live forever, so she was shocked when in Rome during May 1983, Pope John Paul II looked at her with worry. "You look very tired, Mother. I urge you to get a medical checkup."

Mother Teresa felt badly about not doing immediately what the pope urged her to do. But she was so busy. How

MOTHER TERESA ON ABORTION:

Many people are very, very concerned with the children of India, with the children of Africa where quite a few die of hunger, and so on. Many people are also concerned about all the violence in this great country of the United States. These concerns are very good. But often these same people are not concerned with the millions who are being killed by the deliberate decision of their own mothers. And this is what is the greatest destroyer of peace today—abortion which brings people to such blindness.

would she find the time? Just three days later in Rome at her house for homeless men on Coelian Hill, a former monastery, she fell out of bed. Pain stabbed her side. At Salvator Mundi Hospital in Rome, the doctors discovered she had a problem worse than a fractured rib. Her heart was failing!

"If you hadn't taken that fall," said the cardiologist, "you would have had a heart attack. Fortunately, this is a condition we can control with medicine. You will still have to use caution. Get rest. Don't use the stairs. In the meantime we are going to keep you here until you get your strength back."

"That strength will never come with just medicine," she said. "I need something more."

Within hours they had set a routine whereby in her hospital room she could mediate uninterrupted for one hour every morning and afternoon on the wonder of Christ's presence. Also, a priest came to celebrate Mass once a day.

During the day Mother Teresa devoted her thoughts to Jesus, often writing down such meditations:

To me, Jesus is my God.
Jesus is my Spouse.
Jesus is my Life.
Jesus is my Love.
Jesus is my all in all.
Jesus is my everything.
Jesus I love with all my heart, with my whole being.
   I have given Him all, even my sins, and He has es-
   poused me to Himself in tenderness and love. Now
   and for life I am the spouse of my crucified Spouse.
   Amen.

Seven weeks later, at age seventy-three, Mother Teresa was back at full speed.

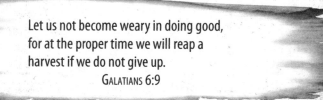

Let us not become weary in doing good, for at the proper time we will reap a harvest if we do not give up.
GALATIANS 6:9

17

"GOD'S WILL BE DONE"

Mother Teresa resumed her demanding role as superior general of the Missionaries of Charity. Yet she knew she had to begin to back off. Organized for some time with six councilors and nineteen regional superiors to help her, for the first time she relinquished her sole responsibility to visit every house. Now her most senior councilors and superiors shared the load.

Of course, she had tried to step down before as superior general. The General Chapter met every six years and voted. Always she was elected by the sisters. Even when she protested. Perhaps she had not been emphatic enough in 1973 and 1979. She would try harder to step down in 1985. Yet Mother Teresa could not desist from the most menial jobs, either. After all, that was a direct favor for Jesus. If the sisters were cleaning a house, Mother Teresa would most likely be doing the most loathsome job of all.

"Cleaning the bathrooms for Jesus," she said with pleasure.

In 1984, she was approached by a priest, suggesting the creation of a congregation of priests bonded to the spirituality and vision of Mother Teresa. He did not know this realized another of her dreams. The Sacred Congregation for the Doctrine of Faith in Rome approved it almost immediately. Weeks later four priests entered a novitiate for the new Missionary Fathers of Charity in a center provided in the Bronx. Mother Teresa told herself that at her age and her condition of health, surely this was her last effort.

"But who am I to say? I am nothing. God's will be done."

By the end of 1984, there were 2,400 sisters in 270 houses, and nearly 500 brothers in 70 houses. The brothers would never grow as the sisters did, because many candidates chose priesthood instead. Due to the deliberately loose organization of the coworkers, their exact numbers were not known. Some said there were now tens of thousands, maybe more than 100,000. Ann Blaikie believed there were 30,000 in England alone.

But the end of the year brought little satisfaction to Mother Teresa. On October 31, she received bitter news. Indira Gandhi, once again India's prime minister, was shot to death by members of her own security guard. Would fighting between factions in India ever cease? Indira's forty-year-old son, Rajiv, would take over as prime minister.

In New Delhi, Mother Teresa stood on the banks of the Jumna River, feeling older than ever. Indira Gandhi, seven years younger, was lying on a sandalwood pyre nearby.

"May her soul live in peace forever," prayed Mother Teresa as the flames consumed her old friend.

In 1985, at the General Chapter, Mother Teresa was once again elected superior general. The sisters wanted none other. The following year she founded Lay Missionaries of Charity, an organization to fill a void between Coworkers and the Missionary Brothers and Sisters. They were rigorously organized religious people who took vows but could marry.

The great event of 1986 was a visit to Calcutta by Pope John Paul II. He was driven directly from the airport to the House of the Dying. It was his way of magnifying the tremendous statement it made to a fast-moving, coldhearted world. There he blessed the destitute, fed their hunger, quenched their thirst. In Rome he had finally given Mother Teresa's poorest of the poor space near the papal palace itself. He often went to the poor there and ministered to their needs.

And so Mother Teresa ceaselessly kept up her mission to the poorest of the poor. Still, in 1989 her heart problems, now accompanied by dangerous fainting spells, caused her to ask the pope for a General Chapter one year ahead of time. At long last, surely she could step down. But no, in 1990 the sisters still voted her in as superior general. At one point Mother Teresa even pleaded with the pope to

MOTHER TERESA ON PRAYING FOR MISSIONARIES:

So you must pray for us that we may be able to be that good news, but we cannot do that without you, you have to do that here in your country.

send out the word to all the cardinals and bishops that she was too old, too tired, to make any more appearances. But no, he had not done that.

Every year now seemed to bring her a bout with heart problems so severe she had to be hospitalized. Her old friend Malcolm Muggeridge succumbed himself in 1990 at age eighty-seven. But Mother Teresa recovered from her problems and rose to serve Christ again and again. She could be no rocking chair superior general. No sooner had she been released from the hospital in 1991 than she rushed immediately to Bangladesh. Its vulnerable swamps facing the sea had once again suffered terrible floods. Food, water, medical care, assistance had to be given as soon as possible to the poorest of the poor! She even traveled to Albania to open a house there. She shrugged. "How could I not do that?"

To not open a house anywhere it was needed, as long as her conditions were met, was unthinkable. This whole-hearted service to the poorest of the poor was her compelling mission. Honors accumulated. Awards. Money.

Honorary degrees. She cared nothing for them. Her Missionaries of Charity had never even compiled a list of them. Time was too precious for such an indulgence. To Mother Teresa, these awards diminished her sacrifice. But still she accepted them. It gave her a chance to deliver her message. Didn't the pope make the same effort? She regarded them as her humiliation.

One of the most glowing tributes came from the Bharatiya Vidya Bhavan organization in India, calling her a "crusader who, in a God-inspired moment, launched a mission of mercy and compassion, reaching out to alleviate the suffering of millions the world over—the nameless, voiceless, homeless, depressed, and dispossessed."[1]

Yes, that tribute humiliated her, too. She had never set out to relieve the suffering millions. It was one person at a time she had helped. Besides, the praise later in their tribute became far too boastful, even false: "She is one of those rare souls who has transcended all barriers of race, religion, creed, and nation. She aspires to no kingdom, no honor, not even salvation."[2] The adulation, the crews of reporters and filmmakers constantly coming to the motherhouse, assumed dimensions far too large.

Rajiv Gandhi was killed in a bombing at an election rally in Madras in 1991. And yet Mother Teresa, in her well-worn eighties, continued on. The numbers of houses and religious and coworkers soared higher and higher. Five hundred centers were in over 100 countries, including nearly 200 centers in India. Sisters numbered over

4,000, coworkers probably over 400,000. Only the brothers were stalled at a few hundred.

New charges were added: battered people, prostitutes, AIDS victims. Old activities continued to expand: 500,000 families fed; 20,000 children taught in 124 schools; 90,000 lepers treated.

One of her greatest legacies was the change in attitude about the poor. The poor were no longer worthless and lazy, many people now admitted. They were valued human beings. It was rare in the 1990s to see the destitute lying unattended, unwanted in the streets of Calcutta. Even children attended these people, if by doing nothing more than to make sure the Missionaries of Charity knew about them. This fulfilled the real need of these destitute: to know they were valued. To be unwanted was the most horrible affliction in the world.

Late in 1996, Mother Teresa at age eighty-six suffered her worst heart attack yet. She underwent her third angioplasty in five years. World press coverage sounded like an obituary. Yet she recovered once again.

That March the sisters finally had shown mercy. They had elected Sister Nirmala as their new mother superior. Sister Nirmala was number seventy-six in the order. Originally from Nepal, she had helped pioneer the contemplative branch of the Missionaries of Charity. She had also served in many countries.

"Please don't call me 'Mother,'" Sister Nirmala insisted sharply at her first press conference.

MOTHER TERESA ON FAMILY:

The family that prays together stays together. . . . Just getting together, loving one another, will bring that peace, that joy, that strength of presence of each other in the home. And we will be able to overcome all the evil that is in the world.

No one had to ask why she said that.

She even came to Washington, D.C., in June 1997, to receive an award from the American Congress. She rose from her wheelchair to remind America that a nation was rich only when it never had too many mouths to feed. And no rich nation found the unborn and the elderly inconvenient.

But the energy was gone. The sly humor and the joy were invisible in her creased face. At long last old age had slowed her to a weak shuffle. There was no way she could shepherd four thousand sisters in 120 countries.

On September 5, 1997, a frail, wheelchair-bound Mother Teresa attended morning Mass in Calcutta with other sisters from the order. As always she felt the real presence of Jesus. Later, pain pulsed in her chest. She refused to be taken from the motherhouse. As hours passed, pain wrenched her chest as never before. Breathing was ever more difficult. By evening she knew God was ending her earthly service to the poorest of the poor. How she wanted to see the face of Jesus. Oh, joy! But this was not dying; this was entering life. Yes, at the age of eighty-seven, Mother Teresa was entering the perfect life, eternal communion with Jesus.

Tributes immediately began pouring in from political and religious leaders around the world. India's government declared a day of mourning and, in a break with tradition, announced she would receive a state funeral. But perhaps the greatest tribute to the "little flower" from Albania was the thousands of nameless mourners who walked and rode buses for hours simply to pay their respects to a woman who had devoted her life to serving Jesus by caring for the poorest of the poor.

"Well done, good and faithful servant! You have been faithful with a few things; I will put you in charge of many things. Come and share your master's happiness!"
MATTHEW 25:21

FURTHER READING

BIOGRAPHIES

Chawla, Navin. *Mother Teresa*. London: Sinclair-Stevenson, 1992.

Doig, Desmond. *Mother Teresa: Her People and Her Work*. New York: Harper & Row, 1976.

Egan, Eileen. *Such a Vision of the Street*. New York: Doubleday, 1985.

Le Joly, Edward. *Mother Teresa of Calcutta*. San Francisco: Harper & Row, 1983.

Muggeridge, Malcolm. *Something Beautiful for God*. New York: Harper & Row, 1971.

Porter, David. *Mother Teresa: The Early Years*. London: SPCK, 1986. Based on Lush Gjergji's Albanian biography.

Spink, Kathryn. *The Miracle of Love*. New York: Harper & Row, 1981.

BOOKS CONTAINING SOME OF MOTHER TERESA'S WRITINGS

Mother Teresa. *Heart of Joy*. Ann Arbor, MI: Servant, 1987.

————. *The Mother Teresa Reader*. compiled by LaVonne Neff. Ann Arbor, MI: Servant, 1995.

————. *A Simple Path*. New York: Random House, 1995.

NOTES

CHAPTER 3
[1] Excerpts taken from *Mother Teresa: The Early Years,* by David Porter. Reprinted with permission from SPCK, London.

CHAPTER 4
[1] Excerpts taken from *Mother Teresa: The Early Years,* by David Porter. Reprinted with permission from SPCK, London.

CHAPTER 5
[1] Excerpts taken from *Mother Teresa: The Early Years,* by David Porter. Reprinted with permission from SPCK, London.
[2] Ibid.
[3] Ibid.
[4] Ibid.

CHAPTER 6
[1] Excerpts taken from *The Life of Mahatma Gandhi,* by Louis Fischer. Reprinted with permission from Harper & Row, New York.

CHAPTER 7
[1] Excerpts taken from *Mother Teresa,* by Navin Chawla. Reprinted with permission from Sinclair-Stevenson, UK.
[2] Ibid.
[3] Ibid.

CHAPTER 8

[1]Excerpts taken from *Mother Teresa*, by Navin Chawla. Reprinted
   with permission from Random House, UK.
[2]Ibid.
[3]Excerpts taken from *Mother Teresa: The Early Years*, by David Porter.
   Reprinted with permission from SPCK, London.
[4]Excerpts taken from *Mother Teresa*, by Navin Chawla. Reprinted
   with permission from Random House, UK.

CHAPTER 10

[1]Excerpts taken from *Mother Teresa of Calcutta*, by Edward Le Joly.
   Reprinted with permission from Harper & Row, San Francisco.

CHAPTER 14

[1]Excerpts taken from *Something Beautiful for God*, by Malcolm
   Muggeridge. Reprinted with permission from Harper & Row,
   New York.
[2]Ibid.
[3]Ibid.

CHAPTER 15

[1]Excerpts taken from *The Miracle of Love*, by Kathryn Spink. Reprinted
   with permission from Harper & Row, New York.

CHAPTER 16

[1]Excerpts taken from *The Miracle of Love*, by Kathryn Spink. Reprinted
   with permission from Harper & Row, New York.

CHAPTER 17

[1]Excerpts taken from *Mother Teresa*, by Navin Chawla.
   Reprinted with permission from Sinclair-Stevenson, UK.
[2]Ibid.

INDEX OF EXCERPTS